CONSTITUTIONAL CRIMINAL PROCEDURE

SECOND EDITION

by

ANDREW E. TASLITZ
Professor of Law
Howard University School of Law

MARGARET L. PARIS
Dean
University of Oregon School of Law

LENESE C. HERBERT
Professor of Law
Albany Law School

2006 Supplement

FOUNDATION PRESS
New York, New York
2006

This publication was created to provide you with accurate and authoritative information concerning the subject matter covered; however, this publication was not necessarily prepared by persons licensed to practice law in a particular jurisdiction. The publisher is not engaged in rendering legal or other professional advice and this publication is not a substitute for the advice of an attorney. If you require legal or other expert advice, you should seek the services of a competent attorney or other professional.

Nothing contained herein is intended or written to be used for the purposes of 1) avoiding penalties imposed under the federal Internal Revenue Code, or 2) promoting, marketing or recommending to another party any transaction or matter addressed herein.

© 2005 FOUNDATION PRESS
© 2006 By FOUNDATION PRESS
      395 Hudson Street
      New York, NY 10014
      Phone Toll Free 1–877–888–1330
      Fax (212) 367–6799
      foundation–press.com
Printed in the United States of America

ISBN–13: 978–1–59941–160–6
ISBN–10: 1–59941–160–1

 TEXT IS PRINTED ON 10% POST CONSUMER RECYCLED PAPER

PREFACE

Since the Second Edition was published in 2003, the United States Supreme Court has added to its jurisprudence on many issues covered in that book. Among other things, it has decided several significant cases arising out of the war in Iraq and the events of September 11, 2001. This supplement includes all pertinent Supreme Court opinions issued up to its 2006 summer recess. It also contains a small sampling of scholarly writings that have illuminated the study of criminal procedure between 2003 and summer 2006.

We are grateful to Robert Kaiser, at the University of Oregon School of Law, for his work on this Supplement.

Andy Taslitz
Margie Paris
Lenese Herbert

July 2006

TABLE OF CONTENTS

TABLE OF CASES   *ix*

Chapter 2   Searches and Seizures:
**   Basic Concepts**   **3**

II.   What is a "Search"?   3
         C.   Factors in *Katz* Analysis   3
                 1.   Location, Location, Location   3
                         Problem 2-3(A)   3
                 3.   Other Factors in Search Analysis   5
                         d. Legality and Intimacy of
                             Activities   5
                             Problem 2-14(A)   8
                         f. Reduced Expectations of Privacy   8
VI.   Searches and Seizures Outside of
         United States Territory   9
VII.   Reasonableness Balancing: An Introduction
         and Sliding Scales   14
         B.   The Limits of Reasonableness
                 Balancing   14
VIII.   "Probable Cause"   17
         A.   Short History of "Probable Cause"   17
                 1.   Quantifying Probable Cause   17
                 2.   Probable Cause as an Objective,
                         Usually Individualized, Determ-
                         ination that Turns on the
                         Collective Knowledge of Law
                         Enforcement   26
         B.   Proving Probable Cause: The *Gates* Test   26
                 4.   The Problem with Informants,
                         Revisited: Informants and
                         Wrongful Convictions   26

**Chapter 3   Searches and Seizures:
                Warrants and Detentions   31**

I.   Warrant Content   31
        B.   Particularity   31
                Problem 3-1(A)   37
        D.   Anticipatory Search Warrants   38
                Problem 3-1(B)   48
II.   Executing the Warrant   48
        B.   Time and Manner of Execution   48
        C.   Treatment of Individuals During
                Warrant Executions   51
III.   Computer Searches   52
        Problem 3-5(A)   55
IV.   Arrests   56
        A.   The Requirement of Reasonableness   56
                3.   Warrant Requirement   56
V.   Stop and Frisk   57
        B.   Defining the Levels of Interaction   57
                1.   Voluntary Encounters Versus
                        Seizures   57
                2.   Stops Versus Arrests   64
                        b. Place of Detention   64

**Chapter 4   Searches and Seizures:
                Warrant Exceptions   66**

I.   Warrantless Searches and Seizures   66
        B.   Six Categories of Warrantless
                Searches and Seizures   66
                1.   Searches Incident to Arrest   66
                        b. Application to Automobiles   66
                5.   "Special Needs" Searches and
                        Seizures   69
                        c. Recognized Areas of Special
                           Needs   69
                           (iv) Searches of Probationers and
                                Probationers' Residences 69
                           (vi) Roadblocks   76
                6.   Consent   80

| | | a. Requirement of Voluntariness | 80 |

Chapter 6   Searches and Seizures:
Terrorism, Surveillance, and
Special Statutory Powers   93

III.		Statutory Regulation of Surveillance	93
	F.	Other Special Statutory Powers	93
		2. Material Witness Warrants	93
	G.	Extended Detention of Persons in the War on Terrorism	102

Chapter 7   Searches and Seizures:
The Exclusionary Rule   113

II.		Limitations on Excluding the Fruits of the Poisonous Tree	113
	C.	Attenuation of the Taint	113
III.		Exceptions to the Exclusionary Rule	126
	A.	The Good Faith Exception	126
	D.	Habeas Review of Violations of the Fourth Amendment Exclusionary Rule	134

Chapter 8   Confessions and Self-Incrimination   135

I.		Due Process and Voluntariness	135
	B.	The Totality of Circumstances Test and its Multiple Goals	135
		1. Reducing the Risk of Unreliable Confessions	135
	F-1.	Does Torture Violate the Due Process Clause?	137
		1. The Question	137
		2. Substantive Due Process	138
		3. Fourth Amendment Prohibition Against Unreasonable Searches and Seizures	144
		4. Eighth Amendment Ban on Cruel and Unusual Punishments	145
		5. International Law	145

			6.	The Problem of Extraterritoriality	146
II.	Custodial Interrogation and the *Miranda* Doctrine				146
	B.	The *Miranda* Decision and Interpretive Controversy			147
			2.	Criticizing and Questioning *Miranda*	147
				c. "Involuntariness" versus "Compulsion"	147
			3.	Affirming *Miranda's* Constitutional Status	148
	C.	*Miranda's* Impact			149
	D.	*Miranda* Thresholds: Custody and Interrogation			148
			1.	The Definition of Custody	149
			2.	The Definition of Interrogation	155
	G.	Scope of the *Miranda* Exclusionary Rule			160
			1.	Fruit of the Poisonous Tree	160
III.	The Sixth Amendment Right to Counsel				164
	C.	Thresholds: Formal Charge and Deliberate Elicitation			164
			2.	Deliberate Elicitation	165
	D.	Invoking and Waiving Sixth Amendment Rights			165
	F.	Scope of the Sixth Amendment Exclusionary Rule			166
IV.	Confessions and Habeas Proceedings				167
	Problem 8-49				168

Chapter 9   Self-Incrimination Outside the Interrogation Room   172

| I. | General Principles of Fifth Amendment Privilege | | 172 |
| | D. | Thresholds: Compulsion, Incrimination, Testimony | 172 |

Chapter 11   The Right to Counsel   174

III.	Effective Assistance of Counsel		174
	A.	The *Strickland* Test	174
	C.	The Workload Problem	178

TABLE OF CASES

References are to Pages.

Berkemer v. McCarty, 468 U.S. 420 (1984), 61, 62

Brigham City v. Charles W. Stuart, 2006 U.S. LEXIS 4155 (2006), 68, 69

Caplin & Drysdale, Chartered v. United States, 491 U.S. 617 (1989), 176

Center for National Security Studies v. U.S. Dept. of Justice, 331 F.3d 918 (D.C. Cir. 2003), 98, 99, 100, 101

Chavez v. Martinez, 538 U.S. 760 (2003), 138, 139, 140, 141, 142, 143, 148, 172

City of Indianapolis v. Edmond, 531 U.S. 32 (2000), 77

Devenpeck v. Alford, 125 S.Ct. 588 (2004), 26

Fellers v. United States, 540 U.S. 519 (2004), 165, 166, 167

Florida v. Nixon, 125 S.Ct. 551 (2004), 175

Garcetti v. Ceballos, 126 S.Ct. 1951 (2006), 27, 28

Georgia v. Scott Fitz Randolph, 126 S.Ct. 1515 (March 22, 2006), 83, 84, 85, 86, 87, 88, 89, 90, 91, 92

Graham v. Connor, 490 U.S. 386 (1989), 144

Groh v. Ramirez, 540 U.S. 551 (2004), 15, 16, 31, 32, 33, 34, 35, 36, 37, 46, 126, 127, 128, 129, 130, 131, 132, 133

Hamdan v. Rumsfeld, 2006 U.S. LEXIS 5185 at *60 (June 29, 2006), 109, 110, 111, 112

Hamdi v. Rumsfeld, 542 U.S. 507 (2004), 100, 101, 102, 103, 104, 105, 106, 107

Hayes v. Florida, 470 U.S. 811 (1985), 56, 57, 81

Hiibel v. Sixth Judicial District Court of Nevada, 542 U.S. 177 (2004), 57, 58, 59, 60, 61, 62, 155, 156, 157, 158, 159

Hudson v. Michigan, 547 U.S. __ (2006)(slip op.), 51, 116, 117, 118, 119, 120, 121, 122, 123, 124

Illinois v. Caballes, 125 S.Ct. 834 (2005), 5, 6, 7

Illinois v. Lidster, 540 U.S. 419 (2004), 76, 77, 78, 79

Illinois v. Wardlow, 528 U.S. 119 (2000), 61, 62

Ingraham v. Wright, 430 U.S. 651 (1977), 145

Iowa v. Tovar, 541 U.S. 77 (2004), 165

Johnson v. Eisentrager, 339 U.S. 763 (1950), 108, 109

Kaupp v. Texas, 538 U.S. 626 (2003), 28, 29, 56, 63, 64, 65, 80, 81, 82, 113, 114, 115

Maryland v. Pringle, 540 U.S. 366 (2003), 17, 18, 19, 20, 21, 22, 23, 24

Minnesota v. Olson, 495 U.S. 91 (1990), 84, 85

Missouri v. Seibert, 542 U.S. 600 (2004), 148, 159, 161, 162, 163, 164

Muehler v. Mena, 125 S.Ct. 1465 (2005), 7, 51, 52

Rasul v. Bush, 542 U.S. 466 (2004), 108, 109

Rompilla v. Beard, 125 S.Ct. 2456 (2005), 175

Rumsfeld v. Padilla, 542 U.S. 426 (2004), 107, 108

Samson v. California, Brief for the Petitioner, 2004 U.S. Briefs 9728, 2005 U.S. S. Ct. Briefs LEXIS 885 (2006), 72, 73, 74, 75, 76

Sanchez-Llamas v. Oregon, 2006 U.S. LEXIS 5177 (2006), 149

Stone v. Powell, 428 U.S. 465 (1976), 134, 166, 167

Thornton v. United States, 541 U.S. 615 (2004), 66, 67, 68

United States v. Arvizu, 534 U.S. 266 (2002), 50

United States v. Banks, 540 U.S. 31 (2003), 48, 49, 50, 51

United States v. Cuauhtemoc Gonzalez-Lopez, 2006 U.S. LEXIS 5165 (June 26, 2006), 175, 176, 177, 178

United States v. Flores Montano, 541 U.S. 149 (2004), 10, 11, 12, 13

United States v. Grubbs, 126 S. Ct. 1494 (2006), 41, 42, 43, 44, 45, 46, 47

United States v. Mendenhall, 446 U.S. 544 (1980), 64

United States v. Patane, 542 U.S. 630 (2004), 148, 160, 161, 162

United States v. Verdugo-Urquidez, 494 U.S. 259 (1990), 144, 146

Wiggins v. Smith, 539 U.S. 510 (2003), 174, 175

Withrow v. Williams, 507 U.S. 680 (1993), 166, 167

Yaborough v. Alvarado, 541 U.S. 652 (2004), 149, 150, 151, 152, 153, 154, 155

Ybarra v. Illinois, 444 U.S. 85 (1979), 21

Zadvydas v. Davis, 533 U.S. 678 (2001), 146

2006 SUPPLEMENT

CONSTITUTIONAL CRIMINAL PROCEDURE

SECOND EDITION

CHAPTER 2

SEARCHES AND SEIZURES: BASIC CONCEPTS

II. WHAT IS A "SEARCH"?

C. FACTORS IN *KATZ* ANALYSIS

1. LOCATION, LOCATION, LOCATION

Page 116. Insert the following after Problem 2-3:

PROBLEM 2-3(A)

In January the Drug Enforcement Administration ("DEA") and State Police investigated and prosecuted an organization involved in manufacturing large quantities of methamphetamines. Some members of the organization cooperated with law enforcement by identifying other members that had not yet been prosecuted, including Mr. Pibb. Mr. Pibb's involvement was confirmed using phone records establishing that he communicated with other confirmed members of the organization.

On March 23, sheriff deputies found 2,000 empty pseudoephedrine bottles with the bottoms cut open. From his extensive training in DEA seminars and twelve years experience in the narcotics division of the State Police, Detective Carbon knew that pseudoephedrine was an ingredient for manufacturing methamphetamines and that cutting out the bottoms of bottles was common practice in the manufacture of methamphetamines. The bottles were found near a fence on the corner of Soda Pop Farm, which was subsequently determined to belong to Mr. Pibb.

DEA agents and Detective Carbon began investigating Mr. Pibb and observed him purchasing Methyl-Sulfonyl-Methane ("MSM"), a cutting agent for methamphetamine, on several occasions and in large quantities. They also learned that Mr. Pibb was part owner of Soda Pop Farm, although his place of residence was across town. After conducting surveillance of the farm over a dozen times, agents determined that no one resided at the property, as trucks arrived in the morning and left after dark. Also, there was no movement or activity after the trucks left the property at night. Neighbors told the agents that they did not know if anyone lived on the property.

In September, Special Agent Mann and Detective Carbon entered Soda Pop Farm without a warrant or consent from the owners. On the property, they found a travel trailer, a metal-framed structure with a vinyl covering that was popped open, and an old pickup with a canopy. Detective Carbon peered inside the canopy and saw large pails labeled MSM, a propane burner, blenders, plastic gloves, and pots. Inside the metal structure, agents found a long stick with a red stain on one end. Detective Carbon knew from his experience that red phosphorus was an ingredient used to make methamphetamines and that materials seen in the canopy window are commonly used to make the drug. Agents also found glass lids similar to those seized from the Organization. The agents did not enter the travel trailer, but did shine a flashlight into the window. The interior was dirty and contained four propane tanks. The countertops were empty and there was an old foam pad but no bedding or personal effects. There were no electrical power lines leading to the trailer.

A week later, the surveillance team observed Mr. Pibb's truck at Soda Pop Farm and heard noises coming from the metal structure that sounded like the movement of pots and pans. Mr. Pibb left the farm after dark and arrived at his house across town shortly thereafter. The next day, Detective Carbon submitted an affidavit of his findings to a judge and obtained a warrant to search Mr. Pibb's residence across town, his truck, and Soda Pop Farm. Subsequently, Mr. Pibb was arrested and charged with manufacturing methamphetamine.

Question: First determine whether the doctrines of curtilage and/or open fields apply. Second, assume that you are Mr. Pibb's attorney. What arguments would you make to suppress the evidence seized pursuant to the warrant? Third, how would prosecutors argue that law enforcement established probable cause to obtain a warrant? Finally, what facts, if any (besides a confession), would help to ensure that the motion to suppress would be denied?

3.   OTHER FACTORS IN THE SEARCH ANALYSIS

d.   Legality and Intimacy of Activities

Page 138. Insert the following before "Vantage Point":

In *Illinois v. Caballes*,[1] the Court followed the reasoning of both *Jacobsen* and *Place* in holding that a drug dog sniff of a lawfully-seized car did not violate the Fourth Amendment. In the ten minutes it took one officer to effectuate the routine traffic stop, a second officer walked his drug dog around Caballes's car, searched the car after the dog alerted, and found marijuana. Caballes was arrested and convicted for narcotics offenses. The Court reasoned that the drug dog sniff did not prolong the length of the lawful stop beyond what was "justified by the traffic offense and the ordinary inquiries incident to such a stop." Therefore, the stop could only have violated the Fourth Amendment if the use of the dog unconstitutionally expanded the scope of the stop.

The Court found that the dog sniff was not a search, and therefore did not unconstitutionally expand the scope of the lawful traffic stop. In reaffirming the holding of *Place* that a drug dog sniff is treated as *"sui generis"* and not a search under the Fourth Amendment, the Court pointed to the teachings of *Jacobsen*: "governmental conduct that *only* reveals the possession of contraband 'compromises no legitimate privacy interest.'"[2]

Justice Souter argued in his dissent that a dog sniff should

---

[1] 543 U.S. 405 (2005).
[2] *Id.* at 408.

not be classified as "*sui generis*" and should be treated as a Fourth Amendment search. According to Souter, "[t]he classification [of a dog sniff as "*sui generis*"] rests ... on a ... premise that experience has shown to be untenable, the assumption that trained sniffing dogs do not err."[3] Studies have shown that drug dogs have an error rate between seven and 60 percent. Souter went on to say that the dog sniff search of Caballes's car was not reasonable because the police did not have probable cause to believe that Caballes was violating a drug law.

Souter also argued that *Jacobsen* is distinct from *Caballes* in that the plaintiff in *Jacobsen* did not have a privacy interest in cocaine that was already lawfully in police possession. Dissimilarly, in *Caballes*, the dog alert merely "informe[ed] the police ... of a reasonable chance of finding contraband they have yet to put their hands on, so the certainty and limit on disclosure that may [have] follow[ed] [were] missing."[4]

Justice Ginsburg's dissent, which Justice Souter joined, argued that dog sniffs should be subject to the two-part *Terry* test. Ginsburg wrote that she "would apply *Terry*'s reasonable-relation test, as the Illinois Supreme Court did, to determine whether the canine sniff impermissibly expanded the scope of the initially valid seizure of Caballes."[5] Ginsburg concluded that because the "expansion of the seizure here from a routine traffic stop to a drug investigation broadened the scope of the investigation in a manner that ... runs afoul of the Fourth Amendment."[6] She also pointed out that injecting such an intimidating animal as a drug dog "change[d] the character of the encounter" in a way that deserves Fourth Amendment protection.

Finally, Ginsburg argued that the majority's decision has dealt a serious blow to Fourth Amendment protection from unreasonable searches. "Under today's decision," she wrote, "every traffic stop could become an occasion to call in the dogs, to the distress and embarrassment of the law-abiding population."

---

[3] *Id.* at 410 (Souter, J., dissenting).

[4] *Id.* at 416 (Souter, J., dissenting).

[5] *Id.* at 422 (Ginsburg, J., dissenting).

[6] *Id.* at 420 (Ginsburg, J., dissenting).

Furthermore, the Court's decision "clears the way for suspicionless, dog-accompanied drug sweeps of parked cars along sidewalks and in parking lots."[7]

Using reasoning similar to that of the majority in *Caballes*, the United States Supreme Court held in *Muehler v. Mena*[8] that when police executing a search warrant questioned a resident about her immigration status, they did not expand the scope of the search. The *Muehler* petitioners were lead officers of a police detachment executing a warrant to search for gang-related contraband in a residence that respondent *Mena* shared with several others. Officers handcuffed her for the duration of the search, and while she was handcuffed, they questioned her about her immigration status. She sued the officers, alleging (among other things) that their questioning violated her Fourth Amendment rights. The Court rejected her claim, emphasizing that the questioning did not extend the duration of the search. Furthermore, the Court observed that "mere police questioning does not constitute a seizure."

Several state courts have interpreted their states' constitutions so as to impose greater limitations on police actions. This is particularly true in the area of dog sniffs. For example, several years after the United States Supreme Court issued its opinion in *Place*, the Court of Appeals of New York held that dog sniffs are searches under New York's constitution.[9] Said that court, "[u]nlike the Supreme Court, we believe that the fact that a given investigative procedure can disclose only evidence of criminality should have little bearing on whether it constitutes a search." The New York court did hold, however, that a dog sniff was minimally intrusive and needed to be justified only by reasonable suspicion, as opposed to probable cause. In 2003, the Montana Supreme Court found a search where police led a dog around a suspected drug dealer's car, which was parked in a public parking lot.[10] The dog alerted to the trunk, which was searched and resulted in a prosecution. The Montana court reasoned that the dealer had put

---

[7] *Id.* at 422 (Ginsburg, J., dissenting).
[8] 544 U.S. 93 (2005).
[9] *State v. Dunn*, 563 N.Y.S.2d 388 (1990).
[10] *State v. Tackitt*, 67 P.3d 295 (2003).

items into his trunk to keep them private. This expectation, said the court, had been interfered with and hence a search had occurred.

PROBLEM 2-14(A)

Having received reliable information that Marsha was manufacturing methamphetamine in her kitchen, police obtained a warrant to search her house for drugs. At the same time, the IRS believed that Marsha had committed tax fraud, and it sent two of its agents to accompany police as they executed the warrant. Believing their safety to be at risk whenever they worked on drug cases, the police handcuffed Marsha as they entered her house. While she was handcuffed, the IRS agents questioned her about her taxes. She claimed that she had never done anything wrong but that she couldn't answer their questions completely, explaining that "it's all complicated, and I'd have to check the files over there." The agents opened the cabinet to which Marsha had inclined her head and located several files labeled "Tax Returns." A thorough analysis indicated that Marsha's returns were accurate. Did the IRS agents violate Marsha's Fourth Amendment rights when they questioned her? When they searched her cabinet and read her files?

f.   Reduced Expectations of Privacy

Page 142. Insert the following before "Subpoenas":

Given the factors set out in section II(C) of this chapter, do you think the Supreme Court will (or should) treat states' taking individuals' DNA as a search? While "appellate courts in this country are virtually unanimous in upholding statutes [that require taking DNA from certain categories of convicted persons,]"[11] Professor Tracey Maclin argues that the Court will likely find that states' forcibly obtaining and testing DNA samples of arrestees constitutes a search under the Fourth Amendment for three reasons.[12]

---

[11] *Nason v. State*, 102 P.3d 962 at 694 (Alaska Ct. App. 2004) (citing cases).
[12] Tracey Maclin, *Is Obtaining an Arrestee's DNA a Valid Special Needs Search Under the Fourth Amendment? What Should (and Will) the Supreme Court Do?*, 33 J. L. MED. & ETHICS 102 (2005).

According to Maclin, although an individual's DNA is exposed to the public, the Court will likely follow the holding of *Kyllo v. United States* – "a search occurs when government agents use sense-enhancing technology to collect any information ... that could not otherwise be obtained without a physical invasion." DNA sampling and analysis certainly uses sense-enhancing technology and is therefore a search. Also, "[a]ny physical intrusion into the body ... constitutes a search for Fourth Amendment proposes. ... Therefore, although DNA sampling can be accomplished in a minimally invasive manner by testing epithelial cells, the odds are very good that the court will conclude that the taking and analysis of the sample is a search under the Fourth Amendment." Furthermore, "[b]ecause DNA has the potential to reveal a host of private facts about an arrestee, the Court will probably find that forcibly taking and testing DNA is a search."

VI.   SEARCHES AND SEIZURES OUTSIDE OF UNITED STATES TERRITORY

Page 169. Insert the following before Part VII:

Searches outside of United States territory must be compared to searches at the border, to which the Fourth Amendment unquestionably applies, but in a highly attenuated manner given the need to protect the border. There is some degree of ambiguity governing the substance of the search and seizure rules at the border. Understanding the likely rules—and the uncertainty about their meaning—requires distinguishing searches of the person from searches of property and, within the former category, arguably separating "routine" from "non-routine" searches of the person. Routine, suspicionless, warrantless seizures of the person and of property are generally permitted at the border. Here, we do not explore the border search cases in detail but do turn to a recent case in which the Court addressed the rules controlling searches of property at the border and, along the way, summarized and distinguished the rules governing other sorts of border searches, albeit while still leaving much uncertainty in the constitutional doctrinal scheme.

In *United States v. Flores-Montano*,[13] the Court had the opportunity to consider the appropriate scope of a border search. There, customs inspectors removed and disassembled the gas tank of a car entering the United States from Mexico at the international border in Southern California. The inspectors seized 37 kilograms of marijuana from Flores-Montano's gas tank. The gas tank removal procedure and the events leading up to it (including waiting for the mechanic) took about an hour.

Flores-Montano was indicted for unlawfully importing marijuana and for possession of marijuana with intent to distribute. The District Court granted defendant's motion to suppress on the ground that the government needed reasonable suspicion—which it did not rely on—to disassemble the gas tank. The Court of Appeals affirmed, declaring that reasonable suspicion is indeed required for "non-routine" border searches, with the degree of a search's intrusiveness being the "critical factor" in determining whether the search was routine.

The United States Supreme Court reversed, rejecting the reasonable suspicion test. The Court held instead that the "Government's authority to conduct suspicionless inspections at the border includes the authority to remove, disassemble, and reassemble a vehicle's fuel tank."[14] "While it may be true that some searches of property are so destructive as to require a different result," the Court noted, "this was not one of them."[15]

Central to the Court's holding was that a search of property, particularly of a car, rather than of a person, was involved. The Court explained: "Complex balancing tests to determine what is a 'routine' search of a vehicle, as opposed to a more 'intrusive' search of a person, have no place in border searches of vehicles."[16]

After noting its frequent recognition that the Government's

---

[13] 541 U.S. 149 (2004).
[14] *Id.* at 155.
[15] *Id.* at 155-56
[16] *Id.* at 153.

10

interest in preventing unwanted entry of persons or property is at its zenith at the border, the Court found that interest strongly implicated in the case before it:

> That interest in protecting the borders is illustrated in this case by the evidence that smugglers frequently attempt to penetrate our borders with contraband secreted in their automobiles' fuel tank. Over the past 5-1/2 fiscal years, there have been 18,788 vehicle drug seizures at the Southern California ports of entry.... Of those, 18,788, gas tank drug seizures have accounted for 4,619 of the vehicle drug seizures, or approximately 25%. ... In addition, instances of persons smuggled in and around gas tank components are discovered at the ports of entry of San Ysidro and Otay Mesa at a rate averaging 1 approximately every 10 days.[17]

The Court concluded that Flores-Montano's privacy interest was small, the expectation of privacy being "less at the border than it is in the interior."[18] The Court noted that it had long recognized that automobiles seeking to enter the United States may be searched. Said the Court, "It is difficult to imagine how the search of a gas tank, which should be solely a repository for fuel, could be more of an invasion of privacy than the search of the automobile's passenger compartment."[19]

But, argued Flores-Montano, the Fourth Amendment "protects property as well as privacy."[20] Granted, said the Court, but noting, in an incredulous tone, that on this record he "cannot truly contend that the procedure of removal, disassembly, and reassembly of the fuel tank in this case or any other has resulted in serious damage to, or destruction of, property."[21] Indeed, noted the Court, in the 348 gas tank searches in which no contraband was

---

[17] *Id.* at 154-55.
[18] *Id.* at 155.
[19] *Id.*
[20] *Id.*
[21] *Id.*

found during fiscal year 2003, the vehicles continued on their way into the country without incident. Moreover, emphasized the Court, Flores-Montano cited not one accident in the many thousands of border gas tank disassembly cases. His reliance on exploratory drilling cases was therefore misplaced, explained the Court, for gas tank disassembly was obviously a very different situation from "potentially destructive drilling," though the Court made clear that it was leaving for another day the question whether, and under what circumstances, a border search of property might be unreasonable because of the "particularly offensive manner"[22] in which it was carried out. Finally, the Court readily dismissed Flores-Montano's claimed right not to be subjected to delay at the international border, finding no case supporting such a right, but also noting that a delay of one to two hours (the Government conceding at oral argument that gas tank searches could take up to two hours) was to be expected at the international border.

Justice Breyer offered a brief concurring opinion, which reads in its entirety as follows:

> I join the Court's opinion in full. I also note that Customs keeps track of the border searches its agents conduct, including the reasons for the searches. This administrative process should help minimize concerns that gas tank searches might be undertaken in an abusive manner.[23]

Notes and Questions

1.   How important was empirical data to the Court's opinion, that is, what if the Court had lacked any data on the number of border searches or their consequences? Could that have affected the outcome of the case? When should such empirical data about the broader history and impact of search and seizure practices and rules play a role in broader Fourth Amendment search and seizure doctrine more generally? For what sorts of purposes might such

---

[22] *Id.* at 155 n.2.
[23] *Id.* at 156 (Breyer, J., concurring).

data be relevant? Should anecdote count, or only supposedly "hard" statistical evidence? Social science research? Who should have the burden of offering such data: the state or the defendant?

2.   Does Justice Breyer's concurring opinion suggest that the state may sometimes have a duty to create data-collection systems concerning the nature and impact of search and seizure practices and policies, at least in the sense that the existence of such systems may be a relevant factor in determining whether a search is reasonable? If so, can requiring the state to collect data on the racial identity of persons searched and seized and the intrusiveness and results of those activities be constitutionally mandated as a way to combat racial profiling? What would be the real-world costs and benefits of such a racial identity data-collection system?

3.   If it is relevant to Fourth Amendment analysis that empirical data exists concerning a search and seizure practice's historical success or failure in discovering and preventing crime, does that mean that other data is relevant as well? For example, should the Court consider relevant a practice's history of disparate racial impact? Does it matter whether the Court has declared that officers' subjective racial animus has no role in the reasonableness determination? Would the result in *Flores-Montano* have been different if there was evidence of an unjustified disparate racial or ethnic impact—for example, that only cars driven by Latinos were selected for gas tank disassembly?

4.   Whether a search is "routine" or not seems still to matter for searches of the person. What criteria should be used to distinguish routine from non-routine border searches? How should the terms "routine" and "non-routine" be defined? What purpose does this routine/non-routine distinction serve, and why is that purpose not served for property searches, according to the Court? "Intrusiveness" still seems to matter in determining the reasonableness of property searches at the border. Does or should intrusiveness be an important factor in defining what is "routine" for searches of the person? Should the routine nature of a search of property be relevant in determining how intrusive the search is, even if the absence of a property search's "routine" nature is not determinative after *Flores-Montano?*

VII. REASONABLENESS BALANCING: AN INTRODUCTION AND SLIDING SCALES

B. THE LIMITS OF REASONABLENESS BALANCING

Page 177. Insert the following before *Concluding Comment*:

As we note in the text on page 9, the text of the Fourth Amendment is less than crystal clear. One of the most difficult questions that it leaves unanswered is this: does the amendment's warrant clause modify its reasonableness clause—in other words, is a search without a warrant, or without probable cause, presumptively unreasonable? We further explain in the text (on page 169) that the Court traditionally has applied a bright-line rule to determine the relationship between the Fourth Amendment's warrant clause and its reasonableness clause. That bright-line rule states that where the government engages in law enforcement searches, it must satisfy the warrant clause's requirements—by obtaining a valid warrant or acting pursuant to a recognized warrant exception—before a search can be found to have been reasonable.

To put this another way, in traditional law enforcement searches the Court engages *not* in reasonableness balancing, but in categorical balancing—invalidating searches if the warrant requirement is not satisfied, or a recognized exception to that requirement is not met, despite case-specific indicia of reasonableness. Unlike *Whren*, then, this is a situation in which categorical balancing favors individual interests over those of law enforcement.

Some justices would like to rebalance these interests by decoupling the warrant clause from the reasonableness clause. If the two clauses were decoupled, a valid warrant would no longer be the presumptive requirement. Rather, whether a warrant is required would turn on a case-specific inquiry into what "reasonableness" demands in the particular circumstances of the case. Indeed, according to these justices, the bright-line rule we describe above has never been as bright as is claimed. Justice Thomas recently stated that the Court "has vacillated between imposing a categorical warrant requirement and applying a general reasonableness standard." The statement came in his dissent in *Groh v. Ramirez*,[24] where a majority of the Court held a search unconstitutional because it was based on an obviously invalid warrant. According to the majority in that case, a residential search is presumed to be unconstitutional if based on an invalid warrant. Categorical balancing applies, in other words, and the individual interests are held categorically to outbalance those of law enforcement. But Justice Thomas, joined by Justice Scalia and the Chief Justice in dissent, suggested in *Groh* that the Court has and should engage in case-by-case reasonableness balancing in these situations:

> The Fourth Amendment provides: "The right of the people to be secure in their persons, houses, papers, and effects, against unreasonable searches and seizures, shall not be violated, and no Warrants shall issue, but upon probable cause, supported by Oath or affirmation, and particularly describing the place to be searched, and the persons or things to be seized." The precise relationship between the Amendment's Warrant Clause and Unreasonableness Clause is unclear. But neither Clause explicitly requires a warrant. While "it is of course textually possible to consider [a warrant requirement] implicit within the requirement of reasonableness," the text of the Fourth Amendment certainly does not mandate this result. Nor does the Amendment's history, which is clear as to the Amendment's principal target (general warrants), but not as clear with respect to when warrants were required, if ever. Indeed, because of the very different nature and scope of federal authority and ability to conduct searches and arrests at the founding, it is possible that neither the history of the Fourth Amendment nor the common law provides

---

[24] 540 U.S. 551 (2004) (Thomas, J., dissenting).

much guidance.

As a result, the Court has vacillated between imposing a categorical warrant requirement and applying a general reasonableness standard. The Court has most frequently held that warrantless searches are presumptively unreasonable, but has also found a plethora of exceptions to presumptive unreasonableness. That is, our cases stand for the illuminating proposition that warrantless searches are per se unreasonable, except, of course, when they are not.

... I would turn to first principles in order to determine the relationship between the Warrant Clause and the Unreasonableness Clause. ...

The view expressed in Justice Thomas's dissent, that the Court has not (and should not) rely on categorical balancing to invalidate searches where the warrant clause is not satisfied, does not yet carry the day. In his majority opinion, Justice Stevens insisted that the Court's "cases have firmly established the basic principle of Fourth Amendment law that searches and seizures inside a home without a warrant are *presumptively* unreasonable."[25]

We will discuss the *Groh* case in more detail later in this supplement. In the meantime, consider these questions:

1.   Based on what you have read about the Fourth Amendment's text and about other tools with which courts interpret that amendment, should the Court employ categorical balancing where the warrant clause is not satisfied, or should it engage in case-by-case reasonableness balancing?

2.   If the Court abandoned categorical balancing for case-by-case reasonableness balancing in the warrant clause context, would you expect outcomes to change – in other words, would

---

[25] 540 U.S. 551 (2004) (emphasis added).

reasonableness balancing result in more pro-law enforcement decisions or more pro-defendant decisions?

VIII. "PROBABLE CAUSE"

A. A SHORT HISTORY OF "PROBABLE CAUSE"

Page 179. Insert the following heading just before the last paragraph at the bottom of the page:

1. QUANTIFYING PROBABLE CAUSE

Page 181. Insert after the second line from the top of the page the following:

The Court may have muddied the quantification question further in *Maryland v. Pringle*,[26] despite the Court's unanimous opinion there. Understanding why this is so first requires examining the lower court opinion for comparison. In *Pringle*, an officer stopped a car for speeding at about 3:00 a.m. There were three occupants in the car: the driver and owner; the front-seat passenger, Joseph Jermaine Pringle; and a back-seat passenger. When the driver, in response to the officer's request to produce his license and registration, opened the glove compartment, the officer saw inside it a large amount of rolled-up cash. When the computer check revealed no outstanding violations, the officer asked the driver to get out, issued him an oral warning, and a second patrol car arrived. The driver, in answering the officer's question on the point, denied having weapons or narcotics in the car and next consented to a vehicle search. That search uncovered $763 from the glove compartment and five glassine plastic baggies containing cocaine from behind the back-seat armrest. As the Court of Appeals of Maryland explained:

> The armrest in the back seat was the type that goes up and down. At the time of the stop, the armrest was in the upright position and flat against the seat.

---

[26] 540 U.S. 366 (2003).

When Officer Snyder pulled down the armrest he found the drugs, which had been placed between the armrest and the back seat of the car and, absent the pulling down of the armrest, *were not visible*.[27]

The officer questioned all three men, telling them that he would arrest them all unless someone admitted to ownership of the drugs. None of the men admitted ownership of either the drugs or the money, and all three were arrested and taken to the police station. Later that morning, Pringle waived his *Miranda* rights and gave oral and written confessions that the cocaine was his and that he meant to sell it, though he denied that the other occupants knew anything about the drugs, and they were therefore released.

The trial court denied Pringle's motion to suppress the confession as the fruit of an illegal arrest, concluding that the arrest was done with probable cause. After a jury convicted Pringle of possession of cocaine and possession with intent to distribute it, he appealed his sentence of ten years without the possibility of parole. The Court of Appeals of Maryland reversed, finding insufficient evidence of probable cause. Central to that court's decision was the absence of evidence that the drugs, and, for that matter, the money, were visible to all occupants before the officer stopped the car. Probable cause for an arrest, explained that court, had to involve adequate proof that Pringle specifically committed the crimes of simple possession and possession with intent to sell. The substantive criminal law of Maryland concerning "possession" required proof that Pringle knew that the drugs were present and that the defendant singly or jointly exercised an actual or potential restraining or directing influence over the drugs, that is, had dominion and control over them. Although the court relied primarily on cases on the sufficiency of the evidence to take the possession question to the jury at trial, the court recognized that probable cause involved a significantly lower "quantum" of evidence. Nevertheless, concluded the Maryland Court, there was *no* evidence here available to the officer at the time of the arrest that Pringle was specifically aware of the cocaine's presence, much less of his influence over it; Pringle's mere presence in the car, in

---

[27] *Pringle v. State*, 370 Md. 525, 531 n. 2 (2002) (emphasis added).

close proximity to the cocaine, was insufficiently individualized evidence of *his* wrongdoing. The Maryland Court explained:

> Under respondent's reasoning, if contraband was found in a twelve-passenger van, or perhaps a bus or other kind of vehicle, or even a place, i.e., a movie theater, the police would be permitted to place everyone in such a vehicle or place under arrest until some person confessed to being in possession of the contraband. Simply stated, a policy of arresting everyone until somebody confesses is constitutionally unacceptable.[28]

The state court likewise rejected the relevance of the large wad of money in the glove compartment because the officer also lacked evidence of the money's visibility to Pringle at the time of his arrest. Thus, concluded the Maryland court:

> The money in the case at bar was not in the plain view of the police officer or petitioner; rather it was located in a closed glove compartment and was opened by the car's owner/driver in response to the officer's request for the car's registration. There are insufficient facts that would lead a reasonable person to believe that *petitioner* at the time of his arrest, had prior knowledge of the money or had exercised dominion and control over it. We hold that a police officer's discovery of money in a closed glove compartment and cocaine concealed behind the rear armrest of a car is insufficient to establish probable cause for an arrest of a front seat passenger, who is not the owner or person in control of the vehicle, for possession of the cocaine.[29]

The United State Supreme Court reversed, thoroughly rejecting the logic of the Court of Appeals of Maryland. In doing so, the Court stressed that the "probable-cause standard is

---

[28] *Id.* at 545, n. 12.
[29] *Id.* at 546.

incapable of precise definition or quantification into percentages because it deals with probabilities and depends on the totality of the circumstances."[30] Moreover, "the *quanta* ... of proof appropriate in ordinary judicial proceedings are inapplicable to the decision to issue a warrant.... Finely tuned standards such as proof beyond a reasonable doubt or by a preponderance of the evidence, useful in formal trials, have no place in the [probable-cause] decision.'"[31] Rather, said the Court, it looks at all the events leading up to the arrest to decide whether, "viewed from the standpoint of an objectively reasonable police officer, [they] amount to probable cause."[32] At the same time, the Court recognized that the "long-prevailing standard of probable cause protects citizens from rash and unreasonable interferences with privacy and from unfounded charges of crime, while giving fair leeway for enforcing the law in the community's protection."[33] Moreover, while the probable cause concept is a "fluid," non-technical one, "turning on the assessment of probabilities in particular factual contexts—not readily, or even usefully, reduced to a neat set of legal rules"—"the *belief of guilt must be particularized with respect to the person to be searched or seized*."[34]

The high Court focused not so much on the *visibility* of the drugs and money as on their *accessibility*:

> In this case, Pringle was one of three men riding in a Nissan Maxima at 3:16 a.m. There was $763 of rolled-up cash in the glove compartment *directly in front of Pringle*. Five plastic glassine baggies of cocaine were behind the back-seat armrest and *accessible to all three men*. Upon questioning, the three men failed to offer any information with respect to the ownership of the cocaine or the money.[35]

---

[30] 540 U.S. at 371.

[31] *Id.*

[32] *Id.*

[33] *Id.* at 370.

[34] *Id.* at 371 (emphasis added).

[35] *Id.* at 371-72 (emphasis added).

The Court criticized the state appellate court's declaration that "[m]oney, without more, is innocuous,'"[36] complaining that the state court's "consideration of the money in isolation, rather than as a factor in the totality of the circumstances, is mistaken in light of our precedents."[37] Accordingly, said the Court,

> We think it an entirely reasonable inference from these facts that any or all three of the occupants had knowledge of, and exercised dominion and control over, the cocaine. Thus a reasonable officer could conclude that there was probable cause to believe Pringle committed the crime of possession of cocaine, either solely or jointly.[38]

Finally, the Court rejected Pringle's argument that this was a mere "guilt-by-association case."[39] Pringle relied for this argument in part on *Ybarra v. Illinois*.[40] In *Ybarra*, police executing a warrant to search a tavern and its bartender for evidence of possession of a controlled substance conducted pat down searches of all the customers present, including Ybarra, and seized six tinfoil packets containing heroin from a cigarette pack retrieved from Ybarra's pocket. The Court invalidated the search, stressing that it was based on insufficiently individualized suspicion as to Ybarra and noting that "[a] person's mere propinquity to others independently suspected of criminal activity does not, without more, give rise to probable cause to search that person."[41] The *Pringle* Court distinguished *Ybarra* and another case relied upon by Pringle, *United States v. DiRe*, thus:

> This case is quite different from *Ybarra*. Pringle and his two companions were in a relatively small automobile, not a public tavern. In *Wyoming v. Houghton*, we noted that "a car passenger—

---

[36] *Id.* at 372.
[37] *Id.*
[38] *Id.*
[39] *Id.*
[40] 444 U.S. 85 (1979).
[41] *Id.* at 91.

unlike the unwitting tavern patron in *Ybarra*—will often be engaged in a common enterprise with the driver, and have the same interest in concealing the fruits or the evidence of their wrongdoing." Here we think it was reasonable for the officer to infer a common enterprise among the three men. The quantity of drugs and cash in the car indicated the likelihood of drug dealing, an enterprise to which a dealer would be unlikely to admit an innocent person with the potential to furnish evidence against him.

In *DiRe*, a federal investigator had been told by an informant, Reed, that he was to receive counterfeit gasoline ration coupons from a certain Buttitta at a particular place. The investigator went to the appointed place and saw Reed, the sole occupant of the rear seat of the car, holding gasoline ration coupons. There were two other occupants in the car: Buttitta in the driver's seat and DiRe in the front passenger seat. Reed informed the investigator that Buttitta had given him counterfeit coupons. Thereupon, all three men were arrested and searched. After noting that the officers had no information implicating DiRe and no information pointing to DiRe's possession of coupons, unless presence in the car warranted that inference, we concluded that the officer lacked probable cause to believe that DiRe was involved in the crime. We said "[a]ny inference that everyone on the scene of a crime is a party to it must disappear if the Government singles out the guilty person." No such singling out occurred in this case; none of the three men provided information with respect to the ownership of the cocaine or money.

We hold that the officer had probable cause to believe that Pringle had committed the crime of possession of a controlled substance.[42]

Notes and Questions

1.   The Court's conclusion is that a reasonable inference is warranted that "any *or* all three of the occupants had knowledge of, and exercised dominion and control over, the cocaine." The "or" suggests that the Court is saying that there are two plausible inferences: first, that at least *one* of the occupants possessed the cocaine; second, that all three jointly possessed the cocaine. Approving of the first inference as sufficient for probable cause, as the Court arguably seems to be doing, however, is confusing. Although the Court denies, and has long denied, that probable cause can be quantified, we have seen that both lower court judges and scholars try to do precisely that, and it is hard to see how probable cause can usefully be defined unless we have at least an approximate ballpark range of acceptable degrees of probability, even if the required range might vary with certain circumstances. But the probability that any one of three car occupants possessed the cocaine is 1/3, or 33-1/3%, a degree of confidence more akin to that assigned by judges and scholars to "reasonable suspicion" rather than to probable cause. If this is right, then how can we distinguish "probable cause" from "reasonable suspicion" after *Pringle*? Is the Court implicitly lowering the required degree of probability for both concepts while keeping "reasonable suspicion" as some undefined degree of probability less than "probable cause" but more than mere suspicion?

2.   The alternative inference suggested by the Court—that all three occupants jointly possessed the drugs—would overcome any mathematical concern, for if *all* possess the drugs as if they are one person, then it is logically the same as if there were in fact only one person in the car. The Court has clearly said that mere presence in a location where drugs are found is insufficient to establish probable cause. The influence of joint possession, therefore, seems to turn significantly on the *accessibility* of the money and the drugs to each of the occupants, that is, that each could have physically taken control over the drugs or money. But

---

[42] 540 U.S. at 373-74.

how can the Court make this question turn on "accessibility" when Maryland state law defines possession as *knowing* that the illegal substance is present and that you have some control over it? If what is required is probable cause to believe that a particular crime or crime has been committed, then does not the nature of that belief necessarily turn on relating it to what the elements of the crime require? Or can there simply be "free-floating" probable cause—a belief by the officer that something illegal is going on, but he does not know what? If "free-floating" probable cause is arguably inconsistent with the idea of individualized suspicion, then how can the Court substitute its judgment of the things that must be suspected as to a specific crime for the state's judgment when it defined the elements of the offense?

The dissent to the Court of Appeals of Maryland case chastised that Court's majority for looking to decisions on the sufficiency of the evidence at trial—a higher standard than "probable cause"—for precedent. But the state court majority did so, it maintained, solely to identify the elements of the crimes of possession and possession with intent to sell, readily agreeing that the quantum of proof required for probable cause was much lower than for sufficiency of the evidence. Who was right: the majority or the dissenters?

3.   The Court also found it significant that the occupants were in a "relatively small automobile, not a public tavern," and that a dealer would not likely admit an innocent person into the car in the first place for fear that the former might testify against the dealer. Concerning this second point: (a) How is it any different, if at all, from the "guilt-by-association" inference that the Court rejects?; (b) Does not this point *assume* that the drugs are visible so that the "innocent" occupant would have personal knowledge of the presence of the drugs about which he could testify?; (c) Are there not many plausible scenarios in which an innocent person could find himself in a car with drug possessors, users, or dealers? If there are, what would they be?

Concerning the first point—the small size of the car: (a) Where do we draw the line on size? Is it the physical size of the vehicle—so that a bus with two passengers and a driver, under circumstances where it is obvious that all three are friends, would somehow be different from the *Pringle* case? (b) Or is it the number of passengers and, if yes, again, where do you draw the line? What if there were four passengers? Five? Six? What if it were a mini-van with eight passengers? The state court majority had challenged the logic that there could be probable cause where there was no evidence that it was Pringle himself who possessed the drugs *as an individual* (whether solely or jointly) precisely on the grounds that it would logically entail holding large numbers of people present on a van or a bus where drugs were found on grounds of "probable cause." Who is right on this point—the state court or the Supreme Court?

4. The Supreme Court also considered it a relevant circumstance that none of the car's occupants confessed to the crime before the arrest, thus disabling the officer from "singling out" the guilty person. How is this inference consistent with the Fifth Amendment privilege against self-incrimination? Does not this inference penalize Pringle and his co-occupants for the exercise of that constitutional privilege in that their silence requires them to pay a heavy toll—being arrested? Is it fair to argue as well that the absence of any "singling out" of one or more individuals as wrongdoers is precisely what demonstrates the absence of probable cause, that is, the absence of an adequate degree of *individualized* suspicion?

5. Is the Court changing the meaning of probable cause across-the-board? Altering its meaning (in the sense of the necessary degree of probability) with the circumstances? Not changing its meaning at all? Does the Court's approach give adequate guidance to law enforcement and to lower courts about when and how they should find that probable cause does or does not exist?

2.   ·PROBABLE CAUSE AS AN OBJECTIVE, USUALLY INDIVIDUALIZED, DETERMINATION THAT TURNS ON THE COLLECTIVE KNOWLEDGE OF LAW ENFORCEMENT

[Return to the first full paragraph at the top of p. 181 of the text].
Page 181. Insert the following before second full paragraph:

In *Devenpeck v. Alford*,[43] the United States Supreme Court reaffirmed its stance that probable cause is a highly objective measure. Police in that case had probable cause to arrest Alford for impersonating an officer, but at the time they arrested him they mistakenly believed that he was violating the Washington Privacy Act by making an audio recording of his interaction with them, and in the arrest papers they cited that Act. The Supreme Court upheld the arrest, emphasizing that "an officer's state of mind (except for the facts that he knows) is irrelevant to the existence of probable cause."[44] In other words, because the officers had probable cause to arrest Alford for impersonating an officer, the arrest was legal even though they arrested and intended to charge him on a different offense.

B.   PROVING PROBABLE CAUSE: THE GATES TEST

4.   THE PROBLEM WITH INFORMANTS, REVISITED: INFORMANTS AND WRONGFUL CONVICTIONS

Page 200. Insert the following just before Problem 2-27:

9.   *Warrants and Prosecutor Ethics:*   Richard Ceballos, a supervising deputy district attorney, upon the request of defense counsel, conducted an investigation that led him to conclude that evidence had been obtained by the police pursuant to a search warrant that had been based upon an affidavit containing serious misrepresentations. Ceballos recommended to his superiors that the case be dismissed, but they proceeded with the prosecution. At a

---

[43] 543 U.S. 146 (2004).
[44] *Id.* at 153.

subsequent suppression hearing, Ceballos testified as a witness for the defense. He later filed a lawsuit alleging that his First and Fourteenth Amendment rights had been violated by retaliation against him by his superiors for his efforts to dismiss the case, including reassigning him to a different position and courthouse and denying him a promotion.

In *Garcetti v. Ceballos*,[45] the United States Supreme Court reversed a Ninth Circuit decision that Ceballos had a cause of action, thus letting stand a district court grant of summary judgment against Ceballos. The high Court concluded that Ceballos had no constitutional free speech protection because he spoke pursuant to the duties of his official role as an employee, not his independent status as a citizen, thus being subject to discipline by his employer without violating the First and Fourteenth Amendments. A contrary rule, maintained the Court, would subject managerial discretion to routine judicial oversight, interfering with management's ability to achieve its objectives and failing to recognize the employer's need to have control over what the employer itself has commissioned or created. Furthermore, argued the Court, although exposing governmental inefficiency and misconduct is important, federal and state whistleblower protection laws, labor codes, and, for government attorneys, rules of conduct and constitutional obligation apart from the First Amendment provide ample protection.

Justices Stevens, Souter, and Breyer filed dissenting opinions, with Justices Ginsburg and Stevens joining Souter's dissent. Of particular note is Justice Breyer's view that lawyers, particularly prosecutors, are different from other public employees:

> First, the speech at issue is professional speech – the speech of a lawyer. Such speech is subject to independent regulation by canons of the profession. Those canons provide an obligation to speak in certain instances. And where that is so, the government's own interest in forbidding that speech is diminished.

---

[45] 126 S.Ct. 1951 (2006).

Second, the Constitution itself here imposes speech obligations upon the government's professional employee. A prosecutor has a constitutional obligation to learn of, to preserve, and to communicate with the defense about exculpatory and impeachment evidence in the government's possession.[46]

Does the majority or Justice Breyer have the better of the argument here?

Page 208. Insert the following before Problem 2-32:

Perhaps the facts of a recent United States Supreme Court case, *Kaupp v. Texas*,[47] will help in answering these questions. In *Kaupp*, after police discovered that a missing 14-year-old girl had been having a sexual relationship with her 19-year-old half brother, they questioned her brother at police headquarters. The brother had been in the company of then 17-year-old Kaupp, so he too was brought to headquarters for questioning. Kaupp was cooperative and was allowed to leave. But the brother thrice failed a polygraph examination and eventually confessed to stabbing his half-sister, then placing her body in a drainage ditch. He implicated Kaupp in the crime.

The detectives failed to obtain a "pocket warrant" but brought Kaupp in for further questioning anyway. The Supreme Court later explained the detectives' efforts this way:

The detectives applied to the district attorney's office for a "pocket warrant," which they described as authority to take Kaupp into custody for questioning…. The detectives did not seek a conventional arrest warrant, as they did not believe they had probable cause for Kaupp's arrest…. As the trial court later explained, the detectives had no

---

[46] 126 S.Ct. 1951, 1974-1975 (2006) (Breyer, J., dissenting).
[47] 538 U.S. 626 (2003).

28

evidence or motive to corroborate the brother's allegations of Kaupp's involvement....; the brother had previously failed three polygraph examinations, while, only two days earlier, Kaupp had voluntarily taken and passed one, in which he denied his involvement....[48]

Kaupp, once confronted with the brother's confession, admitted having some part in the crime and was thus indicted, convicted, and eventually sentenced to 55 years' imprisonment. On appeal, the issue that ultimately made it to the Court was whether Kaupp's admissions were the fruit of an arrest without probable cause, an issue discussed later in this Supplement. The important point for now is that neither the detectives nor the state on appeal challenged Kaupp's claim that he had been brought to the station without probable cause. (The state did challenge whether probable cause was required, however, arguing that Kaupp was not "arrested"; alternatively, maintained the state, Kaupp fit within an exception to the exclusionary rule.) Whether these facts established probable cause for an arrest was thus not before the Court, and any statements on that subject would unquestionably be *dicta*. Nevertheless, the "pocket warrants" quote from the Court's opinion excerpted above can arguably be interpreted as expressing the Court's approval of the detectives' own judgment that they in fact lacked probable cause.

Consider: If this interpretation is right, how broadly should that *dicta* be read? Should an uncorroborated statement by a suspect who implicates another in the crime never be sufficient to establish probable cause for the arrest? Was it the polygraph results—showing lies by the informant, but truthful statements by Kaupp—that were the problem? If corroboration is needed, what sort of corroboration and how much? Would evidence of Kaupp's motive for the killing be sufficient, or would more direct evidence of Kaupp's involvement be necessary? When, if ever, would permitting ready use of uncorroborated statements by potential co-defendants create an unacceptable risk of convicting the innocent? Was there such a risk for Kaupp? Could that fear have been

---

[48] *Id.* at 628 n.1.

relevant to the Court's ultimate conclusions?

CHAPTER 3

SEARCHES AND SEIZURES: WARRANTS AND DETENTIONS

I. WARRANT CONTENT

B. PARTICULARITY

Page 242. Insert the following before Problem 3-1:

What happens when the warrant *application* is adequately particular, but the warrant itself fails to include sufficient detail? The Supreme Court recently suggested that unless the warrant expressly incorporates and appends the application, its silence violates the Fourth Amendment. In the situation giving rise to the Court's opinion in *Groh v. Ramirez*[49], Jeff Groh (a Special Agent for the federal Bureau of Alcohol, Tobacco and Firearms) submitted an application for a warrant to search Mr. and Mrs. Joseph Ramirez's Montana ranch for "any automatic firearms or parts of automatic weapons, destructive devices to include but not limited to grenades, grenade launchers, rocket launchers, and any and all receipts pertaining to the purchase or manufacture of automatic weapons or explosive devices or launchers." The warrant itself did not specify these or any other items that law enforcement officers were authorized to seize. Instead, in the particularity portion of the warrant, Groh merely described the Ramirezes' residence. The warrant did not incorporate by reference the items identified in the application. Moreover, the application was not attached to the warrant when it was executed— indeed, it remained in court under seal. Writing for a 5-person majority, Justice Stevens held the warrant invalid, reiterating that "[t]he Fourth Amendment by its terms requires particularity in the

_____

[49] 540 U.S. 551 (2004).

warrant, not in the supporting documents." The requirement serves a "high function," according to Justice Stevens:

> and that high function is not necessarily vindicated when some other document, somewhere, says something about the objects of the search, but the contents of that document are neither known to the person whose home is being searched nor available for her inspection. We do not say that the Fourth Amendment forbids a warrant from cross-referencing other documents. Indeed, most Courts of Appeals have held that a court may construe a warrant with reference to a supporting application or affidavit if the warrant uses appropriate words of incorporation, and if the supporting document accompanies the warrant. But in this case the warrant did not incorporate other documents by reference, nor did either the affidavit or the application (which had been placed under seal) accompany the warrant.

The Court concluded that the warrant "did [not] make what fairly could be characterized as a mere technical mistake or typographical error." Instead, it was "so obviously deficient" that the Court had to regard the subsequent search as "warrantless."

Interestingly, Groh had conceded in the Supreme Court the invalidity of the warrant. Nevertheless, he urged the Court to evaluate the case based on the circumstances in which his search was carried out, rather than to decide it based simply on the presence or absence of a valid warrant. The search, he argued, was reasonable because it was "functionally equivalent to a search authorized by a valid warrant." Among the circumstances viewed by Groh as bearing on the search's reasonableness were (1) the Magistrate's determination that the application established probable cause, (2) the fact that during his execution of the warrant Groh told Mrs. Ramirez what he was looking for, and (3) the fact that Groh's search and seizure did not exceed the particulars contained in the application.

Justice Stevens rejected Groh's efforts to decouple the Fourth Amendment's warrant clause from its reasonableness clause. The Court's cases "have firmly established," he stated, "the basic principle of Fourth Amendment law that searches and seizures inside a home without a warrant are presumptively unreasonable." He explained further that this "presumptive rule against warrantless searches applies with equal force to searches whose only defect is a lack of particularity in the warrant."

Justice Stevens went further to explain that he saw no reason in this situation to deviate from the categorical rule:

> Petitioner asks us to hold that a search conducted pursuant to a warrant lacking particularity should be exempt from the presumption of unreasonableness if the goals served by the particularity requirement are otherwise satisfied. He maintains that the search in this case satisfied those goals—which he says are "to prevent general searches, to prevent the seizure of one thing under a warrant describing another, and to prevent warrants from being issued on vague or dubious information,"—because the scope of the search did not exceed the limits set forth in the application. But unless the particular items described in the affidavit are also set forth in the warrant itself (or at least incorporated by reference, and the affidavit present at the search), there can be no written assurance that the Magistrate actually found probable cause to search for, and to seize, every item mentioned in the affidavit. *See McDonald*, 335 U.S., at 455 ("Absent some grave emergency, the Fourth Amendment has interposed a magistrate between the citizen and the police. This was done ... so that an objective mind might weigh the need to invade [the citizen's] privacy in order to enforce the law"). In this case, for example, it is at least theoretically possible that the Magistrate was satisfied that the search for weapons and explosives was justified by the showing in the affidavit, but not convinced that any

evidentiary basis existed for rummaging through respondents' files and papers for receipts pertaining to the purchase or manufacture of such items. Or, conceivably, the Magistrate might have believed that some of the weapons mentioned in the affidavit could have been lawfully possessed and therefore should not be seized. *See* 26 U.S.C. § 5861 (requiring registration, but not banning possession of, certain firearms). The mere fact that the Magistrate issued a warrant does not necessarily establish that he agreed that the scope of the search should be as broad as the affiant's request. Even though petitioner acted with restraint in conducting the search, "the inescapable fact is that this restraint was imposed by the agents themselves, not by a judicial officer."

We have long held, moreover, that the purpose of the particularity requirement is not limited to the prevention of general searches. A particular warrant also "assures the individual whose property is searched or seized of the lawful authority of the executing officer, his need to search, and the limits of his power to search." *See* ... *Illinois v. Gates*, 462 U.S. 213, 236 (1983) ("[P]ossession of a warrant by officers conducting an arrest or search greatly reduces the perception of unlawful or intrusive police conduct").[*] ...

---

[*] It is true, as petitioner points out, that neither the Fourth Amendment nor Rule 41 of the Federal Rules of Criminal Procedure requires the executing officer to serve the warrant on the owner before commencing the search. Rule 41(f)(3) provides that "[t]he officer executing the warrant must: (A) give a copy of the warrant and a receipt for the property taken to the person from whom, or from whose premises, the property was taken; or (B) leave a copy of the warrant and receipt at the place where the officer took the property." Quite obviously, in some circumstances—a surreptitious search by means of a wiretap, for example, or the search

It is incumbent on the officer executing a search warrant to ensure the search is lawfully authorized and lawfully conducted.[**] Because petitioner did not have in his possession a warrant particularly describing the things he intended to seize, proceeding with the search was clearly "unreasonable" under the Fourth Amendment. The Court of Appeals correctly held that the search was unconstitutional.

In addition to the five justices who joined Justice Stevens's opinion, two others agreed that the Fourth Amendment had been violated. Justices Thomas and Scalia, however, dissented from that holding. Both would decouple the warrant clause from the reasonableness clause and apply reasonableness balancing rather than categorical balancing to situations like the one presented in *Groh*. Moreover, according to Justice Thomas, the search should not be treated as a "warrantless" one:

... [A] search conducted pursuant to a defective

---

of empty or abandoned premises—it will be impracticable or imprudent for the officers to show the warrant in advance. Whether it would be unreasonable to refuse a request to furnish the warrant at the outset of the search when, as in this case, an occupant of the premises is present and poses no threat to the officers' safe and effective performance of their mission, is a question that this case does not present.

[**] The Court of Appeals' decision is consistent with this principle. Petitioner mischaracterizes the court's decision when he contends that it imposed a novel proofreading requirement on officers executing warrants. The court held that officers leading a search team must "mak[e] sure that they have a proper warrant that in fact authorizes the search and seizure they are about to conduct." That is not a duty to proofread; it is, rather, a duty to ensure that the warrant conforms to constitutional requirements.

warrant is constitutionally different from a "warrantless search." Consequently, despite the defective warrant, I would still ask whether this search was unreasonable and would conclude that it was not. ...

"[A]ny Fourth Amendment case may present two separate questions: whether the search was conducted pursuant to a warrant issued in accordance with the second Clause, and, if not, whether it was nevertheless 'reasonable' within the meaning of the first." *United States v. Leon*, 468 U.S. 897, 961 (1984) (STEVENS, J., dissenting). By categorizing the search here to be a "warrantless" one, the Court declines to perform a reasonableness inquiry and ignores the fact that this search is quite different from searches that the Court has considered to be "warrantless" in the past. Our cases involving "warrantless" searches do not generally involve situations in which an officer has obtained a warrant that is later determined to be facially defective, but rather involve situations in which the officers neither sought nor obtained a warrant. By simply treating this case as if no warrant had even been sought or issued, the Court glosses over what should be the key inquiry: whether it is always appropriate to treat a search made pursuant to a warrant that fails to describe particularly the things to be seized as presumptively unreasonable. ...

[I]n contrast to the case of a truly warrantless search, if a warrant (due to a mistake) does not specify on its face the particular items to be seized but the warrant application passed on by the magistrate judge contains such details, a searchee still has the benefit of a determination by a neutral magistrate that there is probable cause to search a particular place and to seize particular items. In such a circumstance, the principal justification for applying a rule of presumptive unreasonableness falls away.

In the instant case, the items to be seized were clearly specified in the warrant application and set forth in the affidavit, both of which were given to the Magistrate. The Magistrate reviewed all of the documents and signed the warrant application and made no adjustment or correction to this application. It is clear that respondents here received the protection of the Warrant Clause. Under these circumstances, I would not hold that any ensuing search constitutes a presumptively unreasonable warrantless search. Instead, I would determine whether, despite the invalid warrant, the resulting search was reasonable and hence constitutional.

Page 242. Insert the following after Problem 3-1:

PROBLEM 3-1(A)

In early 1999, Detective Lewis Drahm of the Elm Grove Police Department began an investigation following the discovery of photographs of a local 14-year-old boy engaged in sexual acts. Drahm was able to locate and interview the boy and his father. The boy told the detective that the photographs were taken during a sexual encounter with a man who contacted him in an Internet chat room. Upon learning of the situation, the victim's father allowed Drahm to transport the family computer to the police department for further investigation and provided permission to access his son's AOL account. The boy provided Drahm with the password. Using the boy's Internet account, Drahm logged on to AOL and received an e-mail from someone with the screen name "Capnjeffry," who was listed in the boy's AOL instant messenger "Buddy List." Following several emails with Capnjeffry in which Drahm posed as the boy, Drahm obtained a warrant to search AOL's records for information regarding Capnjeffry. AOL informed the detective that the screen name "Capnjeffry" belonged to Jeffery Lesinger. After several more email conversations in which Lesinger continued to solicit sex from the boy, Drahm applied for search and arrest warrants, detailing in the warrant applications his investigations to date and identifying the suspected crime as "using or attempting to use the Internet to induce a minor to engage in sexual activity." After obtaining the warrants and arresting Lesinger, Drahm searched Lesinger's computer, discovering numerous pieces of evidence supporting the prosecution.

Lesinger filed a motion to suppress the fruits of the computer search, alleging that the warrant lack sufficient particulars. The warrant specified, among the places to be searched, "computer equipment including computer hard drives, digital and magnetic storage devices, computer printouts, and computer software." Describing the items to be seized, the warrant listed "sexually explicit material or paraphernalia used to lower the inhibition of children, child pornography, material related to past molestation such as photographs, communication with children relating to sexual activity, and journals recording sexual encounters with children." Lesinger contended that the warrant provided insufficient objective limits on where in his computer hard drive the detective was authorized to search. He also claimed that the warrant authorized the seizure of virtually every document and file on his hard drive. Lesinger specifically referenced the Court's decision in *Groh* in his motion—stating that, after *Groh*, a warrant lacks particularity "unless it clearly establishes, through a specific list of places to be searched and items to be seized, the magistrate's control over the scope of the search."

Question: Assume you are the judge evaluating Lesinger's suppression motion. How should you rule? How will you explain the application of *Groh* to Lesinger's situation?

Page 245. Insert the following just before "II. Executing the Warrant."

D.   Anticipatory Search Warrants

Ordinary search warrants are generally based on affidavits establishing probable cause to believe that evidence of a crime is at a specified location at, or shortly before, the time that the affidavit is prepared. The evidence is also expected to be at that location at a later time: the time that the warrant is executed. The Federal Rules of Criminal Procedure indeed require execution of a warrant within no more than ten days precisely to avoid the problem of the warrant's turning "stale,"[50] that is, the passage of time rendering it less likely that the items once there will still be so. Moreover, if officers having a warrant learn that the specified items have left the location before the search actually occurs, they are no longer entitled to execute the warrant because the supposition of continued presence no longer holds.[51]

Anticipatory warrants are instead based on affidavits purportedly establishing probable cause to believe that evidence of crime will be at the specified location at the time of the search. But the affiant does not declare that the items are already there at, or about, the time of the affidavit's preparation. Anticipatory warrants are thus issued based upon more thorough predictions of the future than are traditional warrants. Although traditional warrants do reflect one future supposition – that the evidence will still be there at the time of warrant execution – the basis for issuing the warrant is past-oriented: the evidence was at the location at some point.[52] This relative difference in future orientation raises questions about the constitutionality of anticipatory warrants. Are they ever constitutional? A useful analogy can be made to electronic surveillance warrants, which are also issued based on the belief that conversations will occur in the future, though they may not have occurred in the past. The Court has upheld their constitutionality under certain conditions that refine the probable cause and warrant requirements to limit police discretion in this more amorphous (relative to traditional warrants) situation, and Congress has passed legislation to implement the Court's conditions (these matters are discussed in detail in a forthcoming

---

[50] *See* FED. R. CRIM. P. 41 (E)(2)(A); *United States v. Wagner* , 989 F. 2d 69, 75 (2d Cir. 1993) (staleness).

[51] *See, e.g., United States v. Bowling*, 900 F. 2d 926, 932 (6h Cir. 1990).

[52] *See* Andrew E. Taslitz, *Fortune-Telling and the Fourth Amendment: Of Terrorism, Slippery Slopes, and Predicting the Future*, 58 RUTGERS L. REV. 195, 202 & n. 31 (2005) (briefly summarizing the nature of anticipatory warrants and the constitutional concerns they raise).

chapter on electronic surveillance).[53] Justice Black's dissent in *Katz* (a case involving warrantless electronic eavesdropping of expected public telephone conversations) captures the constitutional difficulty of future-oriented searches like electronic ones:

> [T]he language of the second clause indicates that the [Fourth] Amendment refers not only to something tangible so it can be seized but to something already in existence so it can be described. Yet the Court's interpretation would have the Amendment apply to overhearing future conversations which by their very nature are nonexistent until they take place. How can one "describe" a future conversation, and, if one cannot, how can a magistrate issue a warrant to eavesdrop one in the future? It is argued that information showing what is expected to be said is sufficient to limit the boundaries of what later can be admitted into evidence; but does such general information really meet the specific language of the Amendment which says "particularly describing"? Rather than use language in a completely artificial way, I must conclude that the Fourth Amendment simply does not apply to eavesdropping.[54]

Black's conclusion was that electronic surveillance was constitutional because its future orientation rendered it entirely outside Fourth Amendment regulation, a position that the *Katz* majority implicitly rejected.[55] Yet Black's analysis mattered even more if the Amendment does apply: How do we gauge probable cause when we are fortune-telling the future? How do you describe what does not exist? The Court and Congress have offered detailed answers to those questions in the electronic surveillance context. But anticipatory warrants seek to extend this future orientation to all evidence, including ordinary physical evidence. Does the

---

[53] *See id.* at 201-02 (summarizing the statutory and case law).

[54] *Katz v. United States*, 389 U.S. 347, 365-66 (Black, J., dissenting).

[55] *See* Taslitz, *Fortune-Telling, supra* note 52, at 201-02.

Fourth Amendment ever permit such an extension and, if so, under what conditions?

Lower courts have mostly said "yes" to the constitutionality of the extension but have often required a strong guarantee that the affiant's prediction will indeed come to pass, for example, requiring probable cause to believe that contraband is on a "sure course" to its intended destination. These courts have also often specified "triggering conditions" – post-warrant events that must come to pass before the anticipatory warrant may actually be executed, such as actually seeing a package ultimately delivered to a home that fits the warrant description of the expected package.[56] The United States Supreme Court recently had its first opportunity to weigh in on these questions of the constitutionality of anticipatory warrants in *United States v. Grubbs*.[57]

Jeffrey Grubbs had been arrested pursuant to a federal search warrant of his home on the basis of an anticipatory warrant issued by a magistrate judge, the affidavit of which indicated that the warrant was only to be executed after a "controlled delivery" of contraband to Grubbs' home. The contraband was a videotape of child pornography that he had ordered from an undercover federal postal inspector via the Internet. The warrant affidavit clearly recited a triggering condition:

> [e]xecution of this search warrant will not occur unless and until the parcel has been received by a person(s) and has been physically taken into the residence . . . . At that time, and not before, this search warrant will be executed by me and other United States Postal inspectors, with appropriate assistance from other law enforcement officers in accordance with this warrant's command.[58]

The affidavit also contained two attachments describing Grubbs' home and the items to be seized. These attachments were incorporated into the warrant, though the affidavit was not. The

---

[56] *See id.* at 202 &n. 31-32.
[57] 126 S. Ct. 1494 (2006).
[58] *Id.* at 1497.

affidavit mentioned the attachments, however:

> "Based upon the foregoing facts, I respectfully submit there exists probable cause to believe that the items set forth in Attachment B to this affidavit and the search warrant, will be found at [Grubbs' residence], which residence is further described at Attachment A."[59]

Two days later, an undercover postal inspector delivered the package containing the videotape to Grubbs' home; Grubbs' wife signed for the package and took it, unopened, into the home. When Grubbs left his home a few minutes later, police detained him and searched his home. Approximately half an hour into the search, Grubbs was provided a copy of the warrant that included the attachments but not the supporting affidavit containing the warrant's "triggering" condition.

Grubbs subsequently consented to interrogation and admitted ordering the videotape. He was arrested. The videotape and other items were seized. A grand jury indicted him on one count of "receiving a visual depiction of a minor engaged in sexually explicit conduct," a violation of 18 U.S.C. Section 2252(a) (2).[60] Grubbs moved to suppress the evidence, arguing that the warrant was invalid "because it failed to list a triggering condition."[61] Grubbs' motion was denied by the district court; he pleaded guilty, reserving his right to appeal the denial.

On appeal, the Ninth Circuit reversed, holding that the Fourth Amendment's particularity requirement "applies with full force to the conditions precedent to an anticipatory search warrant." The Ninth Circuit reasoned that an anticipatory warrant suffering from such a defect "may be 'cured' if the conditions precedent are set forth in an affidavit that is incorporated in the warrant and 'presented to the person whose property is being searched.'" Because the postal inspectors "'failed to present the affidavit – the only document in which the triggering conditions

---

[59] *Id.* at 1497.
[60] *Id.* at 1497-98.
[61] *Id.* at 1498.

were listed' – to Grubbs and his wife, the 'warrant was . . . inoperative, and the search was illegal.'"

The Supreme Court granted certiorari based on two challenges to the search warrant: 1) the "antecedent question" of whether anticipatory search warrants are "categorically unconstitutional" (failing to satisfy the Fourth Amendment requirement that "no Warrants shall issue, but upon probable cause") and 2) whether listing the "triggering condition" in the warrant is necessary to "'assure the individual whose property is searched or seized of the lawful authority of the executing officer, his need to search, and the limits of his power to search.'"[62]

The Court, in an opinion authored by Justice Scalia, reversed the Ninth Circuit. In discussing the first question, the Court determined that because probable cause "exists when 'there is a fair probability that contraband or evidence of a crime will be found in a particular place," and because this requirement necessarily "looks to whether evidence will be found when the search is conducted, all warrants are, in a sense, anticipatory."[63] Granted, said the Court, with ordinary warrants police seek authority to search for what is already there. But the magistrate's determination in that ordinary case that there is probable cause for the search nevertheless "amounts to a prediction that the item will still be there when the warrant is executed."[64] The anticipatory aspect of all warrants is even clearer, said the Court, with electronic surveillance. Accordingly, "[a]nticipatory warrants are... no different in principle from ordinary warrants."[65] Moreover (and like ordinary warrants), anticipatory warrants:

> require the magistrate to determine (1) that it is now probable that (2) contraband, evidence of a crime, or a fugitive will be on the described premises (3) when the warrant is executed. It should be noted, however, that where the anticipatory warrant places a condition (other than the mere passage of time)

[62] *Id.* at 1409, 1501.
[63] *Id.* at 1500.
[64] *Id.* at 1499.
[65] *Id.* 1500.

upon its execution, the first of these determinations goes not merely to what will probably be found if the condition is met. (If that were the extent of the probability determination, an anticipatory warrant could be issued for every house in the country, authorizing search and seizure if contraband should be delivered – though for any single location there is no likelihood that contraband will be delivered.) Rather, the probability determination for a conditioned anticipatory warrant looks also to the likelihood that the condition will occur, and thus that a proper object of seizure will be on the described premises. In other words, for a conditioned anticipatory warrant to comply with the Fourth Amendment's requirement of probable cause, two prerequisites of probability must be satisfied. It must be true not only that if the triggering condition occurs "there is a fair probability that contraband or evidence of a crime will be found in a particular place . . ." but also that there is probable cause to believe the triggering condition will occur. The supporting affidavit must provide the magistrate with sufficient information to evaluate both aspects of the probable-cause determination.[66]

Thus, "when an anticipatory warrant is issued, 'the fact that the contraband is not presently located at the place described in the warrant is immaterial, so long as there is probable cause to believe that it will be there when the search warrant is executed.'"[67] Because the anticipatory warrant's affidavit explained that "execution of the search warrant will not occur unless and until the parcel [containing child pornography] has been received by a person(s) and has been physically taken into the residence," execution of the warrant before said triggering condition would give the government "no reason to believe the item described in the warrant could be found at the searched location; by definition,

---

[66] *Id.*

[67] *Id.* at 1499.

44

the triggering condition which establishes probable cause has not yet been satisfied when the warrant is issued." The Court found that the magistrate judge had a substantial basis for concluding that the triggering condition would be satisfied (Grubbs' refusal of delivery of the videotape was deemed "unlikely" by the Court) and the government had probable cause to conduct the search of Grubbs' home, given that the warrant's triggering condition occurred prior to the search warrant's execution.[68]

With respect to Grubbs' assertion that the anticipatory search warrant lacked sufficient particularity, thereby invalidating the government's search, the Court determined that the Fourth Amendment "specifies only two matters that must be 'particularly described' in the warrant": "the place to be searched" and "the persons or things to be seized." It does not address "unenumerated matters" such as "conditions precedent" to a warrant's execution.[69]

Regarding the government's "failure" to present either Grubbs or his wife with a copy of the full warrant containing the triggering condition, the Court noted that there is no such Constitutional requirement of warrant presentment in the Fourth Amendment's particularity provision.

Notes and Questions

1.   Is the Court right that in principle there is no distinction between an ordinary warrant and an anticipatory warrant? If there is such a distinction, does the Court's test adequately address the differences? Does the Court's test seem different from the "on a sure course" test of many lower courts? If yes, how?

2.   Does the absence of an express requirement in the Fourth Amendment's text of a warrant's containing "triggering conditions" necessarily exhaust what may be required in a warrant's text to render a search or seizure pursuant to that warrant "reasonable"? In connection with this question, consider the following language in Justice Souter's opinion in Grubbs

---

[68] *Id.* at 1500.
[69] *Id.* at 1500-01.

concurring in part and concurring in the judgment (Souter being joined by Justices Stevens and Ginsburg):

> The Court notes that a warrant's failure to specify the place to be searched and the objects sought violates an express textual requirement of the Fourth Amendment, whereas the text says nothing about a condition placed by the issuing magistrate on the authorization to search (here, delivery of the package of contraband). That textual difference is, however, no authority for neglecting to specify the point or contingency intended by the magistrate to trigger authorization, and the government should beware of banking on the terms of a warrant without such specification. The notation of a starting date was an established feature even of the objectionable 18th-century writs of assistance…. And it is fair to say that the very word "warrant" in the Fourth Amendment means a statement of authority that sets out the time at which (or, in the case of anticipatory warrants, the condition on which) the authorization begins.[70]

Souter considered including the intended condition in the warrant as necessary to inform an executing officer, who may not have been the one obtaining the warrant, of the magistrate's intended limits on police authority. Souter also suggested that a government officer obtaining what the magistrate says is an anticipatory warrant "must know or should realize when it omits the condition on which authorization depends," thereby depriving the state of raising any good faith exception to the exclusionary rule should the search in fact be executed in a way that exceeds the authority the magistrate intended to confer.[71]

3.   The Ninth Circuit in Grubbs had asserted that a property owner must receive notice of the triggering condition before the

---

[70]*Id..* at 1502 (Souter, J., concurring). Five Justices were thus in the majority and three in the Souter opinion, Justice Alito having taken no part in the decision.

[71] *See id.* (Souter, J., citing *Groh v. Ramirez*, 540 U.S. 551, 554-55, 563 & n.6.).

search or he would "stand no real chance of policing the officers' conduct."[72] The majority noted, however, that this argument "assumes that the executing officer must present the property owner with a copy of the warrant before conducting his search."[73] But, continued the Court, "neither the Fourth Amendment nor Rule 41 of the Federal Rules of Criminal Procedure imposes such a requirement." Said the Court, "[t]he Constitution protects property owners not by giving them license to engage the police in a debate over the basis of the warrant, but by interposing...the 'deliberate, impartial judgment of a judicial officer...between the citizen and the police" and by providing for damages actions and suppression of evidence improperly obtained.[74]

Despite this apparently clear majority statement of a no-warrant-presentment rule, Justice Souter declared that "the right of an owner to demand to see a copy of the warrant before making way for the police" "remains undetermined today."[75] Yet Souter seemed to envision a role for the affected citizen, not only the magistrate, in policing the police, contrary to the vision of relative citizen passivity declared by the majority. Thus, Souter said,

> [I]f a later case holds that the homeowner has a right to inspect the warrant on request, a statement of the condition of authorization would give the owner a right to correct any misapprehension on the police's part that the condition had been met when in fact it had not been. If the police were then to enter anyway without a reasonable (albeit incorrect) justification, the search would certainly be open to serious challenge as unreasonable within the meaning of the Fourth Amendment.[76]

Which vision of the citizenry's role under the Fourth Amendment makes more sense as a matter of constitutional law? As a matter of sound policy to guide the crafting of statutes,

---

[72] 377 F. 3d at 1079 n.9.
[73] 126 S. Ct. at 1501.
[74] *Id.*.
[75] *Id.* at 1503 (Souter, J., concurring).
[76] *Id.*

regulations, or executive policies?

PROBLEM 3-1(B)

Detective John O'Malley received an anonymous phone tip declaring that "Robert Obean at 1408 Luna Drive, Los Angeles, is going to be receiving a visit tomorrow from Paula Birnbaum around 4 p.m.. Paula will just be returning from a trip to Mexico and will have smuggled large quantities of cocaine across the border in plastic bags in her alimentary canal. She will stay at Obean's home until she 'passes' the baggies. I know this because Paula shared this information with her new boyfriend – my brother – promising to shower him with gifts from the money she will receive for her efforts. I don't like seeing my baby brother mixed up in anything like this, so I'm calling you to put a stop to it." O'Malley is uncertain whether he has enough information to get a warrant and turns to you, a new Assistant District Attorney, to advise O'Malley on whether he can get a warrant and what, if any, conditions should be recited in the warrant. Advise him. If you think more investigation is needed, specify what, why, and how. Your supervisor, learning of O'Malley's request, has also asked you to draft a brief set of policy guidelines to regulate when and how your office should obtain anticipatory warrants and what the warrants should provide. Draft those guidelines.

II.   EXECUTING THE WARRANT

B.   TIME AND MANNER OF EXECUTION

Page 252. Insert the following just before Part C:

In *United States v. Banks,*[77] the United States Supreme Court likewise faced the question of how long a period of time the police must wait after knocking and announcing before they may forcibly enter a residence. Agents arrived at Banks's two-bedroom apartment at 2:00 p.m. on a weekday afternoon to execute a search warrant for cocaine. Officers at the front door called out "police

---

[77] 540 U.S. 31 (2003).

search warrant" and rapped hard enough on the door to be heard by officers at the back door. After waiting 15 to 20 seconds with no answer, and, given no indication whether anyone was home, the officers broke down the front door with a battering ram. Banks had been in the shower and did not hear the police knocking and was just exiting the shower as the police entered. Their search produced weapons, crack cocaine, and other evidence of drug dealing. Banks moved to suppress the evidence on the ground that the police waited an unreasonably short time before forcing entry, violating both the Fourth Amendment and the federal knock-and-announce statute.

The District Court denied the motion, and Banks pled guilty while reserving his right to challenge the search on appeal. The Ninth Circuit reversed, ordering suppression, after detailing a list of numerous factors to guide the reasonableness inquiry and dividing the possible knock-and-announce circumstances into four categories, each with its own test of reasonableness, placing the current case in category four, entries in which no exigent circumstances exist and in which forced entry by destruction of property is required. That category, the Circuit Court concluded, mandated an "explicit refusal of admittance or a lapse of an even more substantial amount of time" than for cases in the other three categories.

The United States Supreme Court reversed, rejecting the Ninth Circuit's categorical, multi-factor approach. Said the Court, "it is too hard to invent categories without giving short shrift to details that turn out to be important in a given instance, and without inflating marginal ones."[78] Indeed, continued the Court, "no template is likely to produce sounder results than examining the totality of the circumstances in a given case."[79] There was no evidence that the police knew that Banks was in the shower, and, given the risk that cocaine might be flushed down the toilet or otherwise disposed of quickly, the 15 to 20 second wait was appropriate, even without an express refusal of entry:

---

[78] *Id.* at 36.
[79] *Id.*

On the record here, what matters is the opportunity to get rid of cocaine, which a prudent dealer will keep near a commode or kitchen sink. The significant circumstances include the arrival of the police during the day, when anyone inside would probably have been up and around, and the sufficiency of 15 to 20 seconds for getting to the bathroom or the kitchen to start flushing cocaine down the drain. That is, when circumstances are exigent because a pusher may be near the point of putting his drugs beyond reach, it is imminent disposal, not travel time to the entrance, that governs when the police may reasonably enter.... And 15 to 20 seconds does not seem an unrealistic guess about the time someone would need to get in a position to rid his quarters of cocaine.[80]

In weighing the totality of these case-specific circumstances, the Court applied a reasonable suspicion test, in which the question was whether there was adequate evidence to establish reasonable suspicion of exigent circumstances that therefore required prompt entry. That test was analogous to the one used in determining whether the knock-and-announce requirement could be foregone entirely. Thus the Court stressed that the usual, non-technical, flexible test for reasonable suspicion, which the Court articulated in its preceding term in *United States v. Arvizu*,[81] applied:

[W]e recently disapproved a framework for making reasonable suspicion determinations that attempted to reduce what the [Ninth] Circuit described as "troubling ... uncertainty" in reasonableness analysis, by "describ[ing] and clearly delimit[ing]" an officer's consideration of certain factors.... Here, as in *Arvizu*, the Court of Appeal's overlay of a categorical scheme on the general reasonableness analysis threatens to distort the "totality of the

---

[80] *Id.* at 38.
[81] 534 U.S. 266 (2002).

circumstances" principle, by replacing a stress on revealing facts with [a] resort to pigeonholes.... Attention to cocaine rocks and pianos tells a lot about the chances of their respective disposal and its bearing on reasonable time. Instructions couched in terms like "significant amount of time," and "an even more substantial amount of time" ... tell very little.[82]

Page 252. Insert the following before "C. Treatment of Individuals During Warrant Executions":

Recently, in *Hudson v. Michigan*,[83] however, the United States Supreme Court held that the exclusionary rule does not apply to violations of the knock-and-announce rule, or at least not where the violation is a failure to wait a sufficient amount of time after announcing their presence but before entering. The Court found that the social costs of applying the exclusionary rule in this context outweighed the social benefits. (A more detailed discussion of the case follows in Chapter Seven).

C.   TREATMENT OF INDIVIDUALS DURING WARRANT EXECUTIONS

Page 253. Insert the following just before Problem 3-2:

In some circumstances officers may handcuff home residents during search warrant executions. In *Muehler v. Mena*,[84] the United States Supreme Court upheld against a Fourth Amendment claim the handcuffing of a woman during a two- to three-hour search of her residence. The Court analyzed the situation for its "objective reasonableness," a test that it had articulated in *Graham v. O'Connor* (see pages 271-272 of the text for a discussion of *Graham*). The Court reasoned that law enforcement interests "in not only detaining, but using handcuffs, are at their maximum when, as here, a warrant authorizes a search

---

[82] 540 U.S. at 42.
[83] 547 U.S. __ (2006)(slip op.).
[84] 544 U.S. 93 (2005).

for weapons and a wanted gang member resides on the premises." On the other hand, the individual's interests were less weighty because the restraint constituted a "minor intrusion." Justice Stevens disagreed with the majority's application of the *Graham* test, arguing that it did not give enough weight to the fact that the woman was very small, posed no flight risk to the two armed officers guarding her, and did not appear to be involved with the gang activity under investigation.

III.　COMPUTER SEARCHES

Page 266.　Insert the following before Problem 3-4.

At a time when rules governing the warrant process are struggling to evolve with the requirements of digital evidence searches, Professor Orin S. Kerr argues that "the warrant process must be reformed in light of the new dynamics of computer searches and seizures."[85] While it is clear that courts across the country have been particularly divided as to the appropriate particularity requirements of digital evidence search warrants, Kerr points out four specific doctrinal puzzles that have accompanied the emergence of a two-step digital evidence search:

> First, what should the warrant describe as the property to be seized: the physical hardware seized during the first physical search, or the digital evidence obtained during the electronic search? Second, what should the warrant describe as the place to be searched: the location of the hardware, the hardware itself, or the location where the electronic search will occur? Third, when must the electronic search occur—is the timing governed by the same rules that govern the physical warrant execution, by some other rules, or by no rules at all? And fourth, what recordkeeping requirements apply to the electronic search, and when must seized

---

[85] Orin S. Kerr, *Search Warrants in an Era of Digital Evidence*, 75 MISS. L.J. 85 (2005).

computer equipment be returned?

Focusing on statutory rules rather than the Fourth Amendment, Kerr goes on to "propose a series of changes to the law of the warrant process to update it for the era of digital evidence."

A) *The Thing to Be Seized*
The first change I would propose is to modify Rule 41's current requirement that "[t]he warrant must identify the person or property to be searched, and identify any person or property to be seized." In digital evidence cases, more specific language should be used. The language should require the police to state what physical evidence they plan to seize on-site, and then indicate what kind of evidence that they plan to search for in the subsequent electronic search. In other words, agents should be required to describe the goal for *both* the physical search stage *and* the electronic search stage. ... Under this approach, a computer warrant would require the officers to name the specific evidence they are searching for twice, correlating with the two stages of criminal investigations. ...

B) *The Place to Be Searched*
Statutory warrant rules could also be amended to consider the case of computers in government custody. Alternatively, courts could simply approve descriptions of computers that name the place to be searched as the computer itself, held in the custody of whatever government agency presently held custody of that machine. ...

C) *When Can the Search Be Executed*
Significant changes should be made to Rule 41 and equivalent state provisions to specify when each stage of the two-step warrant process should be executed. ... One obvious change would be to amend [the language of Rule 41(e)(2)(A) and (B)]

to clarify that the 10-day and daytime rules do not apply to the subsequent electronic search. ... More importantly, Rule 41 should be amended to create an express provision, along with specific standards, on the question of when a computer must be searched and when it should be returned. ... The standard should consider ... backlogs and delays at government forensic laboratories ... [and] the government's interest in the property, ... [which sometimes] can be satisfied by generating a bitstream copy of the storage device. ...

In cases where the computer is merely a storage device for evidence, the government should be required to seize the computer, create a bitstream copy of its files, and then return the property to its proper owner in a reasonable period of time such as 30 days. ... When the computer hardware is believed to be a fruit, instrumentality of a crime, or contraband, the warrant should contain a different set of requirements. In these cases, the key question is whether the physical computer storage device already seized *actually* is a fruit, instrumentality of crime, or contraband. ... If the material is discovered on the computer, then the person from whom the property has [sic] taken has no legal right to the property; it need never be returned. ...

D) *What Are the Oversight and Recordkeeping Requirements, and When Must Property Be Returned?*

The question of what record keeping requirements to mandate is difficult to answer at this time because the underlying Fourth Amendment rules remain unclear. ... Until we know more about what Fourth Amendment standards apply, it is too early to settle on the proper Rule 41 standard. ... One rule that does not need to be changed concerns the inventory requirement for the return of the warrant. The inventory requirement is limited to physical hardware, and in my view it should remain so limited. ...

I find [an approach requiring a listing of files that details the file name, creation date, access date, file size, and the location of the file on the disk] problematic. The inventory requirement is designed to make the government accountable and permit judicial review of the warrant process. The suspect needs to know what was taken if he wishes to challenge the seizure. Accessing computer storage devices and compiling a list of each device's contents does not seem to serve this function, however; the owner of the computer knows what is on the storage device, and taking the physical device obviously takes the contents of the device as well. Further, such an inventory requirement would have the perverse effect of expanding the government's power to search the computer. Completing the inventory would enable the government to find out all the file names and sizes of the material on the hard drive, which might then provide clues to unrelated crimes.

Page 267. Insert the following after Problem 3-5:

PROBLEM 3-5(A)

Examine Problem 3-1(A) above. Does the search warrant described in that problem satisfy the "overbreadth" concerns that arise in computer searches, as described in the text?

IV.   ARRESTS

A.   THE REQUIREMENT OF REASONABLENESS

3.   WARRANT REQUIREMENT

Page 270. Insert the following just after the paragraph in text that is supported by note 49:

The Court has suggested in *dicta*, however, that it might consider permitting modestly extended seizures of a person from a home or from the street on less than probable cause, albeit under a narrow set of circumstances. In *Kaupp v. Texas*,[86] discussed in more detail elsewhere in this Supplement, the Court held that three police officers' awakening a 17-year old boy in his bedroom at 3 a.m. with a flashlight, then bringing him handcuffed, shoeless, and in his boxer shorts to a police station in a police car, was a de facto "arrest," thus requiring probable cause. The Court explained: "[W]e have never sustained against Fourth Amendment challenge the involuntary removal of a suspect from his home to a police station and his detention there for investigative purposes ... absent probable cause or judicial authorization."[87] Dropping a footnote at this point, and in the same breath, the Court continued: "We have, however, left open the possibility that, under circumscribed procedure, a court might validly authorize a seizure on less than probable cause when the object is fingerprinting,"[88] citing *Hayes v. Florida*.[89] In *Hayes*, the Court found the *warrantless* transport of a rape suspect to the stationhouse for fingerprinting on less than probable cause violative of the Fourth Amendment. But the Court noted that it did not necessarily bar reasonable suspicion detentions for fingerprinting where the judiciary authorized them by issuing a warrant, even though based on less than probable cause. Sixteen years before *Hayes*, the Court had condemned as unconstitutional a roundup of 25 African-Americans for questioning and

---

[86] 538 U.S. 626 (2003).

[87] *Id.* at 630.

[88] *Id.* at 631.

[89] 470 U.S. 811 (1985).

fingerprinting in an effort to identify a rapist.[90] Again, however, the Court had noted that "because of the unique nature of the fingerprinting process, such detentions might, under narrowly defined circumstances, be found to comply with the Fourth Amendment even though there is no probable cause in the traditional sense."[91] The Court seems to be suggesting that certain sorts of seizures of the person are less intrusive than "arrests," thus requiring only reasonable suspicion, but are more intrusive than "stops," thus requiring judicial supervision via a warrant. The Court's repeatedly returning to this concept, albeit in *dicta*, over the course of 35 years suggests that it may be inviting someone to bring the fingerprint warrant issue before the Court.

Consider: If the Court did approve of fingerprint warrants, would it necessarily follow that warrants for brief detention for DNA testing would also be constitutional? Are fingerprint and DNA warrants consistent with the text of the Fourth Amendment? With any of the other data sources for constitutional interpretation?

V. STOP AND FRISK

B. DEFINING THE LEVELS OF INTERACTION

1. VOLUNTARY ENCOUNTERS VERSUS SEIZURES

Page 306. Insert the following before Problem 3-10:

In *Hiibel v. Sixth Judicial District Court of Nevada,*[92] the Court faced a different sort of question whether a suspect stopped under *Terry* can refuse an officer's request. There, the specific request was for the suspect to identify himself by name. A deputy sheriff had been dispatched to investigate a telephone call by someone who reported seeing a man assault a woman in a red and silver GMAC truck on Grass Valley Road. When the officer arrived on the scene, he found a man standing by a parked truck, a

---

[90] *See Davis v. Mississippi*, 394 U.S. 721 (1969).

[91] *Id.* at 727.

[92] 542 U.S. 177 (2004).

woman sitting inside it, and skid marks in the gravel behind the vehicle, suggesting to the officer that the car had stopped suddenly.

The officer approached the man, who appeared to be intoxicated, and told him that the officer was investigating a report of a fight. The officer requested identification, and the as-yet-unidentified man asked him why he wanted to see it. The officer explained that he was conducting an investigation and wanted to find out who the unidentified man was and what he was doing there. After continued refusals to comply, the man taunted the officer, telling him to arrest the man and take him to jail. After eleven total requests for identification, and the passage of several minutes, and after warning the man that he would be arrested if he continued to refuse to comply, the officer did exactly that.

A Nevada statute authorized any peace officer to detain anyone under circumstances reasonably indicating that he had committed, was committing, or was about to commit a crime; the officer may so detain the person, however, only to ascertain his identity and the suspicious circumstances "surrounding his presence abroad." The statute further obligated the detainee to identify himself but declared that he "may not be compelled to answer any other inquiry of any peace officer."

Relying on this statute, the state charged the man, later identified as Larry Dudley Hiibel, with willfully obstructing a public officer in discharging a legal duty of his office. Hiibel was convicted of this charge, and the Sixth Judicial Circuit affirmed, rejecting Hiibel's Fourth and Fifth Amendment challenges. The Supreme Court of Nevada on further review also rejected the Fourth Amendment challenge, while denying without opinion Hiibel's request for a hearing to resolve his Fifth Amendment challenge. The United States Supreme Court granted certiorari on both issues, though here we address only the Fourth Amendment question (the Fifth Amendment challenge is addressed later in this Supplement). The Court affirmed Hiibel's conviction.

The Court acknowledged that stop-and-identify statutes, like the one before it, could not be unduly vague and must involve an initial stop based on specific, objective facts establishing

58

reasonable suspicion to believe that the suspect was involved in criminal activity. Hiibel's situation, said the Court, involved neither problem but rather whether, under the Fourth Amendment, officers cannot only ask one specific question—what is the suspect's name?—but also coerce an answer to that question upon threat of criminal prosecution. The Court found ample justification for upholding a state legislature's choice to give the police such authority:

> Obtaining a suspect's name in the course of a *Terry* stop serves important government interests. Knowledge of identity may inform an officer that a suspect is wanted for another offense, or has a record of violence or mental disorder. On the other hand, knowing identity may help clear a suspect and allow the police to concentrate their efforts elsewhere. Identity may prove particularly important in cases such as this, where the police are investigating what appears to be a domestic assault. Officers called to investigate domestic disputes need to know whom they are dealing with in order to assess the situation, the threat to their own safety, and possible danger to the potential victim.[93]

The Court brushed aside Hiibel's argument that statements in the Court's earlier opinions, including *Terry* itself, emphasized that a person detained can be questioned but is "not obligated to answer," saying those statements meant only that the Fourth Amendment itself imposed no obligations on the citizen. Here, by contrast, a statute created such an obligation. The statute had "an immediate relation to the purpose, rationale, and practical demands of a *Terry* stop" because the "threat of criminal sanction helps ensure that the request for identity does not become a legal nullity."[94] Nor does the statute significantly add to the intrusiveness of a *Terry* stop: "[T]he Nevada statute does not alter the nature of the stop itself: it does not change its duration … or its location…."[95] Furthermore, explained the Court:

---

[93] *Id.* at 186.
[94] *Id.* at 188.
[95] *Id.*

Petitioner argues that the Nevada statute circumvents the probable cause requirement, in effect allowing an officer to arrest a person for being suspicious. According to petitioner, this creates a risk of arbitrary police conduct that the Fourth Amendment does not permit.... These are familiar concerns; they were central to the opinion in *Papachristou,* and also to the decisions limiting the operation of stop and identify statutes in *Kolender* and *Brown.* Petitioner's concerns are met by the requirement that a *Terry* stop must be justified at its inception and "reasonably related in scope to the circumstances which justified" the initial stop.... Under these principles, an officer may not arrest a suspect for failure to identify himself if the request for identification is not reasonably related to the circumstances justifying the stop. The Court noted a similar limitation in *Hayes,* where it suggested that *Terry* may permit an officer to determine a suspect's identity by compelling the suspect to submit to fingerprinting only if there is "a reasonable basis for believing that fingerprinting will establish or negate the suspect's connection to that crime.".... It is clear in this case that the request for identification was "reasonably related in scope to the circumstances which justified" the stop. The officer's request was a commonsense inquiry, not an effort to obtain an arrest for failure to identify after a *Terry* stop yielded insufficient evidence. The stop, the request, and the State's requirement of a response did not contravene the guarantees of the Fourth Amendment.[96]

Justice Breyer, joined by Justices Souter and Ginsburg in dissent, took the position that *requiring* a suspect to answer an officer's questions—even if only seeking the suspect's name—

---

[96] *Id.* at 188-89.

went beyond the limited intrusion justified by *Terry*.[97] For the dissenters, the precedent was clear. Most particularly, Justice White, in his concurring opinion in *Terry*, said: "Of course, the person stopped is not obliged to answer, answers may not be compelled, and refusal to answer furnishes no basis for an arrest, although it may alert the officer to the need for continued observation."[98] Sixteen years later, in *Berkemer v. McCarty*,[99] the full Court had also declared that "an officer may ask the [*Terry*] detainee a moderate number of questions to determine his identity and try to obtain information confirming or dispelling the officer's suspicions. *But the detainee is not obliged to respond*."[100] Even more recently, in *Illinois v. Wardlow*,[101] the Court explained that allowing officers to stop and question a fleeing person is "quite consistent with the individual's right to go about his business or to stay put and remain silent in the face of police questioning."[102] The dissenters summarized their argument thus:

> This lengthy history—of concurring opinions, of references, and of clear explicit statements—means that the Court's statement in *Berkemer,* while technically *dicta*, is the kind of strong *dicta* that the legal community typically takes as a statement of law. And that law has remained undisturbed for more than 20 years.

> There is no good reason to reject this generation-old statement of the law. There are sound reasons rooted in Fifth Amendment considerations for adhering to the Fourth Amendment legal condition circumscribing police authority to stop an individual against his will.... Administrative considerations also militate against change. Can a state, in addition to requiring a stopped individual to answer "What's your name?"

---

[97] *Id.* at 197-99 (Breyer, J., dissenting).
[98] *Terry*, 392 U.S. at 34.
[99] 468 U.S. 420 (1984).
[100] *Id.* at 439 (emphasis added by *Hiibel* dissenters).
[101] 528 U.S. 119 (2000).
[102] *Id.* at 125.

also require an answer to "What's your license number?" or "Where do you live?" Can a police officer, who must know how to make a *Terry* stop, keep track of the constitutional answers? After all, answers to any of these questions may, or may not, incriminate, depending upon the circumstances.

Indeed, as the majority points out, a name itself—even if it is not "Killer Bill" or "Rough 'em up Harry"—will sometimes provide the police with "a link in the chain of evidence needed to convict the individual of a separate offense."... The majority reserves judgment about whether compulsion is permissible in such instances.... How then is a police officer in the midst of a *Terry* stop to distinguish between the majority's ordinary case and this special case where the majority reserves judgment?

The majority presents no evidence that the rule enunciated by Justice White and then by the *Berkemer* Court, which for nearly a generation has set forth a settled *Terry*-stop condition, has significantly interfered with law enforcement. Nor has the majority presented any other convincing justification for change. I would not begin to erode a clear rule with special exceptions.[103]

Notes and Questions

1.   Are you persuaded by the majority's effort to distinguish *Hiibel* from earlier case law on the ground that *Hiibel* involved a statute mandating the suspect to answer, while no such statute existed in the preceding cases? Or was the *Hiibel* Court in effect overruling clear precedent (though "technically" *dicta*) without admitting that it was doing so? If the latter, why not be candid? Is the dissent correct in arguing that such overruling goes against underlying policies of *stare decisis* as applied to the *Hiibel* facts?

---

[103] *Id.* at 199 (Breyer, J., dissenting).

2. Is there, or should there be, a connection between the Fourth and Fifth Amendments such that Fifth Amendment invasions should be relevant to gauging Fourth Amendment intrusiveness? Should the converse apply, that is, should a finding that a search violates (or does not violate) the Fourth Amendment be relevant to whether there has been a violation of the Fifth Amendment privilege against self-incrimination (a privilege to be studied in detail later)?

3. Twice in one term—in the *Hiibel* case and in *Kaupp v. Texas* (discussed below)—the Court went out of its way to cite *Hayes's* dicta suggesting that warrants to pick someone up solely for fingerprinting may be issued based solely on reasonable suspicion. Could the Court be laying the groundwork for addressing the constitutionality of more highly technological identification techniques than fingerprinting that might be useful in the War on Terrorism? How does this approach of using "reasonable suspicion warrants" under certain circumstances square with the text of the Constitution?

4. Would the analysis have changed if the officer had asked Hiibel specifically for the vehicle's registration papers? Whether Hiibel was carrying a gun and, if so, whether he had a permit to carry it with him? Whether he was married to the woman accompanying him and, if so, whether they were on the same health plan and whether he would produce his health insurance card?

5. There is a debate raging over whether it would be constitutional to require all Americans to carry electronic identification cards, including their name, address, social security number, visa status, passport usage, and medical history on the cards, to aid in the War on Terrorism. What, if anything, does *Hiibel* suggest about the constitutionality of such identification cards?

2. STOPS VERSUS ARRESTS

b. *Place of Detention*

Page 309. Insert the following before "Sufficiency of Facts For Stop and Frisk":

In *Kaupp v. Texas*,[104] the Court reaffirmed its rule that, with very rare exceptions, forcible transportation to police headquarters constitutes an arrest. The Court used the same factors identified in *Mendenhall*[105] for distinguishing voluntary encounters from seizures as also relevant to determining whether a seizure is so intrusive as to constitute an arrest, for which probable cause is required:

> The state does not claim to have had probable cause here, and a straightforward application of the test just mentioned shows beyond cavil that Kaupp was arrested within the meaning of the Fourth Amendment, there being evidence of every one of the probative circumstances mentioned by Justice Stewart in *Mendenhall*. A 17-year-old boy was awakened in his bedroom at three in the morning by at least three police officers, one of whom stated "we need to go and talk." He was taken out in handcuffs without shoes, dressed only in his underwear in January, placed in a patrol car, driven to the scene of the crime and then to the sheriff's offices, where he was taken into an interrogation room and questioned. This evidence points to arrest even more starkly than the facts in *Dunaway v. New York*, where the petitioner "was taken from a neighbor's home to a police car, transported to a police station, and placed in an

---

[104] 538 U.S. 626 (2003). In *dicta*, the *Kaupp* Court left open the possibility of seizure of a person on less than probable cause for fingerprinting.

[105] 446 U.S. 544 (1980). Although the *Mendenhall* opinions were fractured, a majority of the Court approved the *Mendenhall* standards for seizure in *Florida v. Royer*, 460 U.S. 491 (1983).

interrogation room." There we held it clear that the detention was "in important respects indistinguishable from a traditional arrest" and therefore required probable cause or judicial authorization to be legal. The same is, if anything, even clearer here.[106]

---

[106] 538 U.S. at 630-31.

CHAPTER 4

SEARCHES AND SEIZURES: WARRANT EXCEPTIONS

I. WARRANTLESS SEARCHES AND SEIZURES

B. SIX CATEGORIES OF WARRANTLESS SEARCHES AND SEIZURES

1. SEARCHES INCIDENT TO ARREST

b. *Application to Automobiles*

Page 340. Insert the following immediately after the block quote from the Sixth Circuit's decision in *Hudgins*:

The Supreme Court has since disavowed this "initiation rule," however. In *Thornton v. United States*,[107] it held that the *Belton* rule applies regardless of whether the police interaction was initiated before or after the suspect left the vehicle. Instead, the Court adopted a rule linking *Belton's* applicability to temporal and physical proximity between the arrestee and the vehicle, explaining that "the arrest of a suspect who is next to a vehicle presents identical concerns regarding officer safety and the destruction of evidence as the arrest of one who is inside the vehicle." As a result of these concerns, and its desire to maintain a bright-line rule, the Court held that "[s]o long as an arrestee is the sort of 'recent occupant' of a vehicle as petitioner was here, officers may search that vehicle incident to arrest." In the case at hand, Marcus Thornton had pulled into a parking lot and gotten out of his car

---

[107] 541 U.S. 615 (2004).

before a police officer initiated contact with him, although the officer suspected that Thornton had been aware of him and had parked in an effort to evade contact with him.

Despite the clear five-justice majority supporting *Thornton's* holding, the case revealed a surprising amount of disagreement on the Court about *Belton's* continued viability. Justice Scalia concurred in the judgment upholding the search, but he refused to join the Court's opinion and rationale. Justice Scalia would abandon *Belton's* rule and underlying rationales (ensuring officer safety and preventing destruction of evidence), which he viewed as not really at issue in most situations in which *Belton* applies, and substitute this rule: officers may search vehicles upon arrest if they have reason to believe that evidence "relevant to the crime of arrest" might be found in the vehicle. Justice Scalia acknowledged that his proposed rule "is a return to the broader sort of search incident to arrest that we allowed before *Chimel*," but he found support for it in the constitution and in prior case law, and he would limit it "to searches of motor vehicles, a category of 'effects' which give rise to a reduced expectation of privacy." Explaining his proposed rule, he stated:

> There is nothing irrational about broader police authority to search for evidence when and where the perpetrator of a crime is lawfully arrested. The fact of prior lawful arrest distinguishes the arrestee from society at large, and distinguishing a search for evidence of his crime from general rummaging. Moreover, it is not illogical to assume that evidence of a crime is most likely to be found where the suspect was apprehended.

Justice Ginsburg joined Justice Scalia's opinion. Justice O'Connor indicated that she found Scalia's reasoning compelling, but she did not endorse his proposed rule outright because of her "reluctan[ce] to adopt it in the context of a case in which neither the Government nor the petitioner has had a chance to speak to its merit." Justice Stevens, joined by Justice Souter, dissented. He favored retention of the "initiation rule," explaining that *Belton* "is not needed for cases in which the arrestee is first accosted when he is a pedestrian, because *Chimel* itself provides all the guidance that is necessary."

Notes and Questions

1.   The Court's majority was dissatisfied with the fact that the "initiation rule" produced a lack of clarity for police. Does the Court's rule achieve greater clarity in application? What issues, if any, do you anticipate arising in future cases? Do you agree with Justice Stevens that sufficient clarity is provided by applying *Chimel* to situations in which police initiate contact with a suspect after the person has left a vehicle?

2.   Justice Scalia's proposed rule is based in part on a series of cases in which the Court decided that people enjoy reduced expectations of privacy in vehicles. We will discuss those cases later in this chapter. In the meantime, why do you suppose that vehicles are—or should be—accompanied by reduced expectations of privacy?

3.   What consequences would ensue if Justice Scalia's proposed rule were adopted? Does Justice Scalia's rule have a greater bright-line nature than the majority's? Is it more honest, as he claimed?

Page 351. Insert the following just before the final sentence immediately preceding Problem 4-4:

        May police enter a home without a warrant when responding to a 3:00 a.m. noise complaint and, on the scene, witnessing (through the home's kitchen window) a tumultuous fracas that included a landed punch, bloody mouth, and several adults restraining a minor (the puncher)? What if the officer is not interested in breaking up the fight or investigating the situation, but "primarily motivated by intent to arrest and seize evidence?" The Court's answer to both these questions was "yes" in *Brigham City v. Charles W. Stuart*,[108] finding an objectively reasonable basis under these circumstances for police to believe an occupant was

---

[108] 2006 U.S. LEXIS 4155 (May 22, 2006).

seriously injured or imminently threatened with serious injury, thus justifying a warrantless entry into the home, "regardless of an individual officer's state of mind."

In a concurring opinion, Justice Stevens characterized as "peculiar" that despite the Utah trial judge, the intermediate state appellate court, and the Utah Supreme Court all finding a Fourth Amendment violation, "neither trial counsel nor the trial judge bothered to identify the Utah Constitution as an independent basis for the decision because they did not expect the prosecution to appeal."[109] Said Stevens,

> [o]ur holding today addresses only the limitations placed by the Federal Constitution on the search at issue; we have no authority to decide whether the police in this case violated the Utah Constitution.[110]

5.   "SPECIAL NEEDS" SEARCHES AND SEIZURES

(iv)   Searches of Probationers and Probationers' Residences

Page 381. Insert the following before "Searches and Seizures by Customs and Border Patrol Officers":

Should law enforcement be permitted to sample individuals' DNA? "All fifty states currently have legislation requiring that DNA profiles of certain categories of individuals be [created]," and "appellate courts in this country are virtually unanimous in upholding [those] statutes."[111] Some states have "increased the number of individuals eligible for inclusion in these databases" by enacting provisions allowing the taking and analysis of DNA samples from certain categories of arrestees. While the Supreme Court has not addressed the constitutionality of taking DNA samples from persons subject to arrest, Tracey Maclin suggests that "forcibly obtaining and testing DNA samples of arrestees, absent judicial authorization or probable cause for the

---

[109] *Id.* at *17.

[110] *Id.* at *17-18.

[111] *Nason v. State*, 102 P.3d 962, 964 (Alaska Ct. App. 2004).

search, cannot be justified under the special needs exception."[112]

After determining that the Court will likely find that states' forcibly obtaining and testing DNA samples of arrestees constitutes a search under the Fourth Amendment, Maclin goes on to argue that "[b]ecause the so-called 'special needs exception' permits suspicionless searches in a variety of contexts, it would seem to be the most appropriate category for analyzing the constitutionality of taking an arrestee's DNA." However, predicting whether the Court will uphold states' taking arrestees' DNA is not an easy task. "While the Court has issued several rulings under its 'special needs' analysis, these cases do not form a coherent doctrine." Maclin derived four criteria from these rulings that the Court will likely use to determine whether taking arrestees' DNA samples is constitutional. "The criteria include: the purpose of the search; whether law enforcement officials will have access to the results of the search; the extent of police involvement in conducting the search; and finally, whether the search can be characterized as serving civil and criminal law interests." Maclin uses these four criteria to predict whether the Court would uphold taking DNA from arrestees as a valid special needs search.

First, because the purpose behind some states' DNA laws is "to use DNA samples from arrestees to assist law enforcement officials 'in criminal investigations' and to enhance states' 'chances of solving crimes,' such searches would not fit within the special needs exception." Second, many states "make the test results of DNA samples "available directly to federal, and local law-enforcement officers." When law enforcement has access to search results, the Court has been reluctant to uphold those searches under the special needs exception. Third, "the fact that police officials are intimately involved in the implementation of DNA searches strongly suggests that such searches do not satisfy the special needs exception." Finally, "[w]hile DNA searches may advance the states' secondary or ultimate interest in determining the identification of persons held in custody or charged with a

---

[112] See Tracey Maclin, *Is Obtaining an Arrestee's DNA a Valid Special Needs Search Under the Fourth Amendment? What Should (and Will) the Supreme Court Do?*, 33 J.L. MED. & ETHICS 102 (2005).

crime, 'the immediate objective of the searches [is] to generate evidence *for law enforcement purposes …*' Therefore, under the Court's current precedents, forcibly obtaining and testing DNA samples of arrestees … cannot be justified under the special needs exception."

Page 381. Insert the following just before the heading, "(V) Searches and Seizures by Customs and Border Patrol Agents."

Relevant to the question whether individualized suspicion should be required to search probationers and parolees is this underlying inquiry: Are full Fourth Amendment privacy interests restored after a convicted person has completely and successfully served his sentence in accordance with the requirements of his conviction? According to at least one state, the answer is, at best, "not so fast:"

> [t]he California legislature has determined that "the period immediately following incarceration is critical to successful reintegration of the offender into society and to positive citizenship." Cal. Pen. Code § 3000(a)(1). In order to "provide for the supervision of and surveillance of parolees," and "to provide educational, vocational, family and personal counseling necessary to assist parolees in the transition between imprisonment and discharge," California law requires that "[a] sentence pursuant to Section 1168 or 1170 [the general sentencing provisions of the California Penal Code] shall include a period of parole, unless waived as provided in this section."
>
> The period of parole lasts up to three years for certain offenses, and up to five years for others. Id. § 3000(b)(1), (2). If a person receives a life sentence and is subsequently paroled, the period of parole is five years, and may be extended for an additional five years. Id. § 3000(b)(3). In the case of a person sentenced for first or second degree murder, "the period of parole, if parole is granted,

shall be the remainder of the person's life." Id. § 3000.1(a).

Parolees may be discharged from parole before their periods of parole have been completed. Discharge occurs after one year if the parolee was convicted of a nonviolent felony, and after two or three years for most other felonies, unless the Board of Prison Terms determines that the person should be retained on parole for a longer period. Id. § 3001(a), (b). Persons subject to lifetime parole are discharged after five years (in the case of second-degree murder) or seven years (in the case of first-degree murder), unless the Board determines that they should be retained on parole. Id. § 3000.1(b).[113]

The application of parole and its requirements should come as no surprise. However, there is more:

California law provides for a "notice of parole," which is "a general description of rules and regulations governing parole." Cal. Code Regs. tit. 15, § 2511(a). By statute, "the notice of parole shall read as follows: . . . Search. **You and your residence and any property under your control may be searched without a warrant at any time by any agent of the Department of Corrections or any law enforcement officer.**" Id. § 2511(b).[114]

According to the California Supreme Court, "parole is not a matter of choice . . . . there can be no voluntary consent to inclusion of the search condition."[115]

Is this as oppressive as it sounds? Ask Donald Curtis Samson and Deborah Watson:

---

[113] *Samson v. California*, Brief for the Petitioner, 2005 U.S. S. Ct. Briefs LEXIS 885 at *8-10.

[114] *Id.* at *9 (emphasis added).

[115] *People v. Reyes*, 968 P.2d 445, 448 (Cal. 1998) (citation omitted).

On September 6, 2002, at about 5:30 in the afternoon, Officer Alex Rohleder of the San Bruno, California Police Department was driving his patrol vehicle when he observed two adults and a little baby walking down the street. The two adults were Petitioner and his friend Deborah Watson; the baby was Ms. Watson's three-year-old son....Officer Rohleder was not actively looking for Petitioner, but just happened to run across him....Officer Rohleder was aware that Petitioner was on parole, and was under the impression that he might have a parolee at large warrant (issued when a parolee's whereabouts are "unknown" or s/he "remains unavailable for supervision")....The officer conducted a pat-down search of Petitioner for weapons and found nothing. The officer asked Petitioner whether he had an outstanding warrant. Petitioner responded no he didn't....The officer called his dispatcher and confirmed that Petitioner's statements were correct.

The police officer then proceeded to search Petitioner more thoroughly. The officer conducted this second search of Petitioner solely because it's a condition of his parole....Nothing about Petitioner's conduct gave rise to any suspicion that he was engaged in wrongdoing....

The officer explained that, being [a] parolee, Petitioner needs to make sure he's still obeying the laws. It's a privilege for him to be out there. The officer searched Petitioner's pockets and found a cigarette box in his left breast pocket. The officer searched inside the cigarette box and found a plastic baggy containing Methamphetamine.[116]

---

[116] *Samson v. California*, Brief for the Petitioner, U.S. Ct. Briefs LEXIS 885 at *12-13 (internal quotations and citations omitted).

When this case reached the United States Supreme Court, the Court, in an opinion by Justice Scalia, found the search constitutional. Parolees, said the Court, had fewer privacy expectations than probationers because parole is more akin to imprisonment than is probation. A parolee is released *before his sentence of incarceration ends* on condition that he abide by certain rules for the balance of his sentence. A probationer is never incarcerated. Parolees' severely diminished privacy expectations, said the Court, were outweighed by the overwhelming state's interest in supervising parolees because they are so likely to re-offend. The state may not be rendered powerless to combat recidivism by promoting reintegration and positive citizenship, goals that may require privacy intrusions that would not otherwise be tolerated under the Fourth Amendment, maintained the Court. Nor need there be concern about arbitrary application given the state's prohibition on harassing, capricious or arbitrary searches. Additionally, concluded the Court, it was irrelevant that many other states and the federal government require individualized suspicion before searching parolees, for the question is whether the program is drawn to meet California's needs and is reasonable given the parolee's reduced privacy expectations. Said the Court, "The touchstone of the Fourth Amendment is reasonableness, not individualized suspicion."

Justice Stevens, joined by Justices Souter and Breyer in dissent, emphasized that "'[t]he suspicionless search is the very evil the Fourth Amendment was intended to stamp out," and exceptions to its prohibition should be "'jealously guarded,'" limited primarily to special needs searches, yet the Court had not relied on any argument that the parolee search fit the special needs category. Furthermore, the special needs cases required "programmatic safeguards designed to ensure evenhandedness in application; if individualized suspicion is to be jettisoned, it must be replaced with measures to protect against state actors' unfettered discretion." Importantly, Justice Stevens also found the attitudes of the rest of the country, not just Californians, to be critical to the analysis:

> Nor is it enough, in deciding whether someone's expectation of privacy is "legitimate," to rely on the

existence of the offending condition or the individual's notice thereof.... The Court's reasoning in this respect is entirely circular. The mere fact that a particular State refuses to acknowledge a parolee's privacy interest cannot mean that a parolee in that State has no expectation of privacy that society is willing to recognize as legitimate – especially when the measure that invades privacy is both the *subject* of the Fourth Amendment challenge and a clear outlier. With only one or two arguable exceptions, neither the Federal Government nor any other State subjects parolees to searches of the kind to which petitioner was subjected. And the fact of notice hardly cures the circularity; the loss of a subjective expectation of privacy would play "no meaningful role" in analyzing the legitimacy of expectations, for example, "if the Government were suddenly to announce on nationwide television that all homes henceforth would be subject to warrantless entry.[117]

Notes and Questions

1.   The majority and dissenting opinions seem to raise this question: Should what privacy expectations "society" is willing to recognize as reasonable, and the weight of those expectations, be decided based upon the attitudes of "American society" as a whole or the attitudes of those within the state where the search or seizure takes place? Is your answer affected by the Fourth Amendment's statement that the right it recites is one of "the People"? What about each opinion suggests these questions are involved? Are reasonable expectations of privacy and their weight really empirical questions about attitudes, or are they normative questions about what we should expect, or are they both?

2.   What about Ms. Watson, who was in Samson's company at the time of the search?:

---

[117] 2006 LEXIS 4885 at *35 (Stevens, J., dissenting).

The officer also searched Petitioner's companion. . . . According to the officer, Ms. Watson consented to the search. According to Ms. Watson, the officer did not ask permission to search her, but instead told her to empty her pockets and asked if she had any weapons or drugs. After the officer went through Watson's belongings on top of the hood of the car, he told her to go home.[118]

As Ms. Watson was not on parole nor was she a criminal convict, should she have received different treatment? Why? The majority did not consider this precise question but did address a related point: "Likewise, petitioner's concern that California's suspicionless search law frustrates reintegration efforts by permitting intrusions into the privacy interests of third parties is also unavailing because that concern would arise under a suspicion-based regime as well."

(vi) *Roadblocks*

Page 393. Insert the following before Problem 4-19:

The Court's most recent case on this question, *Illinois v. Lidster,*[119] further clarifies the point. In *Lidster*, one week after a fatal hit-and-run accident, police set up a checkpoint to locate witnesses to the crime. As each car approached the checkpoint, an officer would stop the car for 10 to 15 seconds to ask whether its occupants had seen the crime and would hand the driver a flyer asking for assistance. When Robert Lidster approached the checkpoint in his minivan, his van swerved, nearly hitting one of the officers. That officer subsequently smelled alcohol on Lidster's breath, administered a sobriety test, and arrested him. Lidster was convicted of driving under the influence of alcohol and appealed on the ground that much of the evidence against him should have been suppressed as the fruit of an illegal checkpoint seizure. Although the trial court rejected this claim, two Illinois appellate courts accepted it, and the United States Supreme Court accepted

---

[118] *Samson v. California,* Brief for the Petitioner, 2005 U.S. S. Ct. Briefs LEXIS 885 at *14.
[119] 540 U.S. 419 (2004).

certiorari.

At first blush, there was ample reason to support the Illinois appellate court decisions. Unlike in the drunk driving cases, and many of the urine drug-testing cases, there was no imminent danger to public safety, indeed no "civil" purpose at all. The sole reason for the roadblock—one run by the police alone—was to investigate crime. Indeed, the Court had recently held in *City of Indianapolis v. Edmond*,[120] discussed immediately above, that a roadblock to find those transporting—but not necessarily then using—illicit drugs served no immediate safety purpose and was therefore a traditional criminal search requiring probable cause and a warrant or a recognized exception to the warrant requirement.

But, in *Lidster,* the Supreme Court held otherwise, upholding the conviction and the constitutionality of the search. Not all criminal enforcement objectives, explained the Court, are the sort that demand presumptive unconstitutionality absent individualized suspicion. "The stop's primary law enforcement purpose," concluded the Court, was "*not* to determine whether a vehicle's occupants were committing a crime, but to ask vehicle occupants, as members of the public, for their help in providing information about a crime in all likelihood committed by others."[121] The Court continued: "The police expected the information elicited to help them apprehend, not the vehicle's occupants, *but other individuals*."[122] Moreover, in such a situation, requiring individualized suspicion makes no sense, for no individual is stopped because he or she is suspected of, or even potentially sought for, involvement in any crime. "Like certain other forms of police activity, say, crime control or public safety, an information-seeking stop is not the kind of event that involves suspicion, or lack of suspicion, of the relevant individual."[123] Additionally, concluded the Court:

> [I]nformation-seeking highway stops are less likely
> to provoke anxiety or to prove intrusive. The stops

---

[120] 531 U.S. 32 (2000).
[121] 540 U.S. at 419.
[122] *Id*. at 423.
[123] *Id*. at 425.

are likely brief. The police are not likely to ask questions designed to elicit self-incriminating information. And citizens will often react positively when police simply ask for their help as "responsible citizen[s]" to "give whatever information they may have to aid in law enforcement."[124]

Furthermore, said the Court, the law ordinarily allows police to seek voluntary public cooperation in solving crime; the Fourth Amendment "does not treat a motorist's car as his castle"; the traffic delay was brief; and proliferation of similar checkpoints was unlikely given "limited police resources and community hostility to related traffic tie-ups...."[125] Therefore, the Court declared that a more flexible reasonableness balancing test like that in the drunk-driving roadblock cases was appropriate, indeed classifying those latter cases as another example of "special law enforcement concerns ... justify[ing] highway stops without individualized suspicion."[126] The suspicionless, warrantless information roadblock in *Lidster* survived reasonableness balancing because the stop was tailored to serve a grave public concern (finding a killer) in that it was located where there was a good chance of finding drivers knowledgeable about the crime; the delay (including time waiting in a line of cars) was brief—a few minutes at most—and the contact provided little reason for anxiety or alarm, for all cars were temporarily stopped, and there were no allegations of discriminatory or other unlawful police behavior during questioning.

The Court never expressly explained *why* information-seeking stops are less likely to provoke anxiety than many other stops and *why* the *Lidster* stop was more like sobriety checkpoints and even pure public safety measures (like crowd control) than like checkpoints for drug traffickers. Implicitly, however, the level of stigma arguably seemed to be an important factor. A driver stopped to be questioned about witnessing a crime is treated like a respectable citizen rather than a potential criminal. Neither he nor

---

[124] *Id.*

[125] *Id.* at 426.

[126] *Id.* at 424.

knowing observers are likely to see the investigation as even potentially stigmatizing. To the contrary, the Court seems right in suggesting that expecting presumably honest citizens to help in finding the killer of a 70-year-old bicyclist (the hit-and-run driver's victim) is a sign of respect. Categorizing the stop, therefore, as one whose primary purpose was other than the "general interest in crime control" might therefore be correct.

Whether the more flexible resulting balancing test for administrative seizures was met on the *Lidster* facts, however, may be more debatable, as Justice Stevens, joined by Justices Souter and Ginsburg, argued in their opinion concurring in part and dissenting in part. Justice Stevens agreed with the majority's primary purpose analysis but favored a remand for additional factfinding on the application of the reasonableness balancing test. Justice Stevens questioned whether there were less intrusive but equally or even more effective alternatives, such as placing flyers on Post Office employee cars, the victim having just finished work there before the fatal accident. Stevens also questioned whether the annoyance of delay for drivers at a location where many were leaving a factory at the end of a shift and the accompanying large surge of vehicles could be justified by an investigatory method so likely to be ineffective. Because the roadblock was unpublicized, he also speculated that waiting drivers, who would not know the purpose of the search until reaching the checkpoint, might be alarmed at being ensnared in an unexpected midnight roadblock—facts and possibilities entirely ignored by the majority.

Page 394. Insert the following in Problem 4-20, at the end of the current "Question":

Would the roadblock have been justified if, instead of asking permission to search each driver's trunk, the police had asked each occupant of each car whether he or she had any information helpful in finding the snipers? What if the snipers had been caught and the police set up a roadblock questioning vehicle occupants about whether they had information useful in prosecuting and convicting the snipers?

6. CONSENT

a. *Requirement of Voluntariness*

Page 409. Insert the following before the last paragraph:

In *Kaupp v. Texas*,[127] the Court more recently concluded first, that an initial police interaction was non-consensual; second, that, in the alternative, if it was consensual, later events even more clearly were not. *Kaupp* involved a 17-year-old boy suspected of complicity in the murder of a 14-year-old girl. The police admittedly lacked probable cause for an arrest. Nevertheless, they awakened the teenager in his bedroom at 3:00 a.m. with a flashlight, after having been admitted to the boy's home by his father. One of the officers, a Detective Pinkins, identified himself and said, "[W]e need to go and talk."[128] Kaupp said, "Okay." Two officers handcuffed Kaupp, leading him shoeless and in boxer shorts to a police car, driving him to the crime scene, then to the police station, where he admitted some part in the crime.

After his motion to suppress his confession as the fruit of an illegal arrest was denied, he appealed. The Texas Court of Appeals affirmed the conviction, concluding that Kaupp consented to accompany the officers to the crime scene and to the police station. Nor, said the Court of Appeals, was this conclusion altered by Kaupp's being handcuffed and driven to the station in a police car because these practices were "routinely" done to protect officer safety when transporting individuals, and Kaupp "did not resist the use of handcuffs or act in a manner consistent with anything other than full cooperation.'"[129] The Court of Criminal Appeals of Texas denied discretionary review, but the Supreme Court accepted certiorari. The Court rejected the Texas appellate court's conclusion that Kaupp consented to being transported to the police station:

> Kaupp's "Okay" in response to Detective Pinkins statement is no showing of consent under

---

[127] 538 U.S. 626 (2003).
[128] *Id.* at 628.
[129] *Id.* at 629.

the circumstances. Pinkins offered Kaupp no choice, and a group of police officers rousing an adolescent out of bed in the middle of the night with the words "we need to go and talk" presents no option but "to go." There is no reason to think Kaupp's answer was anything more than "a mere submission to a claim of lawful authority."…. If reasonable doubt were possible on this point, the ensuing events would resolve it: removal from one's house in handcuffs on a January night with nothing on but underwear for a trip to a crime scene on the way to an interview room at law enforcement headquarters. Even an "initially consensual encounter…can be transformed into a seizure or detention within the meaning of the Fourth Amendment."…. *See Hayes* ("[A]t some point in the investigative process, police procedures can qualitatively and quantitatively be so intrusive with respect to a suspect's freedom of movement and privacy interests as to trigger the full protection of the Fourth and Fourteenth Amendments"). It cannot seriously be suggested that when the detectives began to question Kaupp, a reasonable person in his situation would have thought he was sitting in the interview room as a matter of choice, free to change his mind and go home to bed.

Nor is it significant, as the state court thought, that the sheriff's department "routinely" transported individuals, including Kaupp on one prior occasion, while handcuffed for [the] safety of the officers, or that Kaupp "did not resist the use of handcuffs or act in any manner consistent with anything other than full cooperation." The test is an objective one, and stressing the officers' motivation of self-protection does not speak to how their actions would reasonably be understood. As for the lack of resistance, failure to struggle with a cohort of deputy sheriffs is *not a waiver of Fourth Amendment protection*, which does not require the perversity of resisting arrest or assaulting a police officer.[130]

Here the Court seems simultaneously to be saying that there was no voluntary consent and that, therefore, a reasonable person in Kaupp's position *would have understood* that he was not free to leave, thus rendering the police action a "seizure"—and a quite intrusive one at that—within the meaning of the Fourth Amendment. Interestingly, though by no means necessary to its decision, the Court here uses "waiver" language, as it also did in *Ferguson*. Yet in *Schneckloth* the Court had rejected waiver— which would require a "knowing, voluntary, and intelligent" relinquishment of rights—as the justification for the consent-to-search doctrine. No one seriously believes that the Court has yet, as a general principle, modified the *Schneckloth* mere "voluntariness" requirement as the sole pre-condition to finding "consent" to search or seize. Still, the application of a waiver test in *Ferguson* and the appearance of waiver language in *dicta* in *Kaupp* may suggest the Court's willingness to move toward the heightened standard of knowing, voluntary, and intelligent "waiver" as the true definition of Fourth Amendment "consent" in some narrow, as-yet-to-be-specified, range of circumstances, even if "consent" remains equated simply with "voluntariness" in the run-of-the-mill case.

---

[130] *Id.* at 631-32 (emphasis added).

Page 413. Insert the following after the second line on the page:

The Supreme Court has recently addressed a similar question in *Georgia v. Scott Fitz Randolph*.[131] In *Randolph*, police responded to a domestic dispute complaint filed by Randolph's estranged wife, Janet, who reported that her husband, a cocaine user, had taken the couple's son. While the police were on the scene, Scott returned, explained that he had removed his son to a neighbor's home to prevent Janet from taking the son out of the country, disputed his wife's accusation regarding the cocaine, and insisted that she was the one with the substance abuse problem.

Once police retrieved the son with Janet's assistance, she renewed her accusations against her husband, adding that there were "items of drug evidence" within their home. Police Sergeant Murphy asked Scott for permission to search the marital home; he unequivocally refused. Sergeant Murphy then asked Janet for permission. Not only did she give permission, she escorted police to a location identified as Scott's bedroom, where a straw with a white powdery substance suspected of being cocaine was discovered. Sergeant Murphy went to his vehicle, where he contacted the local district attorney, who instructed that the search should be stopped and advised Sergeant Murphy to seek a search warrant. Upon Sergeant Murphy's return to the Randolph home, Janet withdrew her consent. Sergeant Murphy seized the straw and the couple, returned to the station, obtained a search warrant, executed the warrant, and subsequently charged Scott with possession of cocaine.

At trial, Scott moved to suppress the evidence. The motion to suppress was denied, on the basis that his wife, Janet, had common authority to consent to the search of their home. The Georgia intermediate and high courts reversed the trial court's denial, noting that Scott's presence and refusal invalidated Janet's consent and made police entry and search of the marital home unreasonable.[132] The Supreme Court granted certiorari to resolve a split in the authority on whether one occupant may give law

---

[131] 126 S.Ct. 1515 (March 22, 2006).
[132] *Id.* at 1519.

enforcement effective consent to search shared premises, as against a co-tenant who is present and announces his refusal to consent to the search.

According to the majority, prior to *Randolph*, the Court had not dealt directly with the reasonableness of police entry "in reliance on consent by one occupant subject to immediate challenge by another:"[133]

> the Fourth Amendment rule ordinarily prohibiting the warrantless entry of a person's house as unreasonable *per se*, ... [has] one "jealously and carefully drawn" exception, *Jones v. United States,* [357 U.S. 493, 499 (1958) which] recognizes the validity of searches with the voluntary consent of an individual possessing authority, *Rodriguez, 497 U.S., at 181...*. That person might be the householder against whom evidence is sought, *Schneckloth v. Bustamonte,*[412 U.S. 218 (1973)], or a fellow occupant who shares common authority over property, when the suspect is absent, *Matlock, supra,* ... and the exception for consent extends even to entries and searches with the permission of a co-occupant whom the police reasonably, but erroneously, believe to possess shared authority as an occupant, *Rodriguez, supra, at 186* .... None of our co-occupant consent-to-search cases, however, has presented the further fact of a second occupant physically present and refusing permission to search, and later moving to suppress evidence so obtained. The significance of such a refusal turns on the underpinnings of the co-occupant consent rule, as recognized since *Matlock.*[134]

According to the majority, however, the Court did take "a step toward the issue" in *Minnesota v. Olson.*[135] There, police arrested Olsen on the basis of evidence that he was involved in the

---

[133] *Id.* at 1522.

[134] *Id.* at 1520.

[135] 495 U.S. 91 (1990).

murder of a gas station attendant. Police arrested Olson in the home of two women with whom he stayed. Olson claimed that police violated his Fourth Amendment expectation of privacy in the women's home when they entered and searched it. There, the Supreme Court held that overnight houseguests have a legitimate expectation of privacy in their temporary quarters because "it is unlikely that [the host] will admit someone who wants to see or meet with the guest over the objection of the guest."[136]

"Longstanding social custom" accepts that those who visit the homes of friends and relatives as temporary, overnight guests have a privacy interest in the premises, based on their status. So, for the majority in *Randolph*, if "that customary expectation of courtesy or deference is a foundation of Fourth Amendment rights of a houseguest, it presumably should follow that an inhabitant of shared premises may claim at least as much, and it turns out that the co-inhabitant naturally has an even stronger claim."[137]

Thus, when the police obtain voluntary consent to search the premises of an occupant who shares (or is reasonably believed to share[138]) common authority over the searched premises and no physically present co-tenant objects, the Fourth Amendment's reasonableness requirement is not offended.

In the present case, however, Scott's presence on the premises and his stated refusal to consent to the warrantless governmental entry and search of the shared home invalidated the government's evidence against him. According to the majority, where a co-tenant is present, vocal, and refusing to consent, police may still decide to enter, search, and seize incriminating evidence as against the consenting co-tenant, but not against the demurring one, over and above that individual's refusal to consent. Justice Souter found persuasive social expectations regarding disputed permission between co-tenants, given that these expectations are a

---

[136] *Id.* at 99.

[137] *Randolph.* 123 S. Ct. at 1522.

[138] *Illinois v. Rodriguez*, 497 U.S. 177 (1990) holds valid warrantless searches where an objectively reasonable police officer would have believed under the circumstances that the consenting party had actual authority to consent to a search, even if s/he did not.

constant element in assessing Fourth Amendment reasonableness in the Court's consent cases:

> [t]o begin with, it is fair to say that a caller standing at the door of shared premises would have no confidence that one occupant's invitation was a sufficiently good reason to enter when a fellow tenant stood there saying, "stay out." Without some very good reason, no sensible person would go inside under those conditions. Fear for the safety of the occupant issuing the invitation, or of someone else inside, would be thought to justify entry, but the justification then would be the personal risk, the threats to life or limb, not the disputed invitation.
>
> ...
>
> The visitor's reticence without some such good reason would show not timidity but a realization that when people living together disagree over the use of their common quarters, a resolution must come through voluntary accommodation, not by appeals to authority. Unless the people living together fall within some recognized hierarchy, like a household of parent and child or barracks housing military personnel of different grades, there is no societal understanding of superior and inferior, a fact reflected in a standard formulation of domestic property law, that "[e]ach cotenant . . . has the right to use and enjoy the entire property as if he or she were the sole owner, limited only by the same right in the other cotenants".... The want of any recognized superior authority among disagreeing tenants is also reflected in the law's response when the disagreements cannot be resolved. The law does not ask who has the better side of the conflict; it simply provides a right to any co-tenant, even the most unreasonable, to obtain a decree partitioning the property (when the relationship is one of co-ownership) and terminating the relationship.... And

while a decree of partition is not the answer to disagreement among rental tenants, this situation resembles co-ownership in lacking the benefit of any understanding that one or the other rental co-tenant has a superior claim to control the use of the quarters they occupy together. In sum, there is no common understanding that one co-tenant generally has a right or authority to prevail over the express wishes of another, whether the issue is the color of the curtains or invitations to outsiders.[139]

...

Since the co-tenant wishing to open the door to a third party has no recognized authority in law or social practice to prevail over a present and objecting co-tenant, his disputed invitation, without more, gives a police officer no better claim to reasonableness in entering than the officer would have in the absence of any consent at all. Accordingly, in the balancing of competing individual and governmental interests entailed by the bar to unreasonable searches, *Camara v. Municipal Court of City and County of San Francisco*,[387 U.S. 523, 536-537(1967)], the cooperative occupant's invitation adds nothing to the government's side to counter the force of an objecting individual's claim to security against the government's intrusion into his dwelling place. Since we hold to the "centuries-old principle of respect for the privacy of the home," *Wilson v. Layne*,[526 U.S. 603 (1999)], "it is beyond dispute that the home is entitled to special protection as the center of the private lives of our people," *Minnesota v. Carter,* [525 U.S. 83 (1998) (Kennedy, J., concurring)]. We have, after all, lived our whole national history with an understanding of "the ancient adage that a man's home is his castle [to the

---

[139] *Randolph,* 123 S. Ct. at 1522-23.

point that t]he poorest man may in his cottage bid defiance to all the forces of the Crown," *Miller v. United States,*[357 U.S. 301 (1958)] (internal quotation marks omitted).[140]

Chief Justice Roberts, along with Justices Thomas and Scalia dissented. The dissenters regarded the issue as a straightforward one, asserting that the Court's cases reflect the understanding that "[e]ven in our most private relationships, our observable actions and possessions are private at the discretion of those around us:"[141]

[i]f an individual shares information, papers, or places with another, he assumes the risk that the other person will in turn share access to that information or those papers or places with the government. And just as an individual who has shared illegal plans or incriminating documents with another cannot interpose an objection when that other person turns the information over to the government, just because the individual happens to be present at the time, so too someone who shares a place with another cannot interpose an objection when that person decides to grant access to the police, simply because the objecting individual happens to be present.[142]

Accordingly, the dissenting Justices would rule as reasonable the warrantless search in Randolph, as the police obtained voluntary consent to enter and search from someone authorized to give it, Scott's wife:

[t]he majority suggests that "widely shared social expectations" are a "constant element in assessing Fourth Amendment reasonableness," ..., but that is not the case; the Fourth Amendment precedents the majority cites refer instead to a "legitimate

---

[140] *Id.* at 1523-24.
[141] *Id.* at 1534 (Roberts, Chief J., dissenting).
[142] *Id.* at 1531 (Roberts, Chief J., dissenting).

expectation of *privacy*...." Whatever social expectation the majority seeks to protect, it is not one of privacy. The very predicate giving rise to the question in cases of shared information, papers, containers, or places is that privacy has been shared with another. Our common social expectations may well be that the other person will not, in turn, share what we have shared with them with another-- including the police--but that is the risk we take in sharing. If two friends share a locker and one keeps contraband inside, he might trust that his friend will not let others look inside. But by sharing private space, privacy has "already been frustrated" with respect to the lockermate.... If two roommates share a computer and one keeps pirated software on a shared drive, he might assume that his roommate will not inform the government. But that person has given up his privacy with respect to his roommate by saving the software on their shared computer.

A wide variety of often subtle social conventions may shape expectations about how we act when another shares with us what is otherwise private, and those conventions go by a variety of labels--courtesy, good manners, custom, protocol, even honor among thieves. The Constitution, however, protects not these but privacy, and once privacy has been shared, the shared information, documents, or places remain private only at the discretion of the confidant.[143]

In addition to balking at the majority's characterization of Court precedent, the dissenting Justices regarded as troubling "costs" of the majority's decision. Specifically, the dissenting minority argued that the Court's decision would thwart abused spouses' consent to warrantless police entry and search of homes which contain nonconsenting criminal spouses:

---

[143] *Id.* at 1533 (Roberts, Chief J., dissenting).

[w]hile the majority's rule protects something random, its consequences are particularly severe. The question presented often arises when innocent cotenants seek to disassociate or protect themselves from ongoing criminal activity.... Under the majority's rule, there will be many cases in which a consenting co-occupant's wish to have the police enter is overridden by an objection from another present co-occupant. What does the majority imagine will happen, in a case in which the consenting co-occupant is concerned about the other's criminal activity, once the door clicks shut? The objecting co-occupant may pause briefly to decide whether to destroy any evidence of wrongdoing or to inflict retribution on the consenting co-occupant first, but there can be little doubt that he will attend to both in short order. It is no answer to say that the consenting co-occupant can depart with the police; remember that it is her home, too, and the other co-occupant's very presence, which allowed him to object, may also prevent the consenting co-occupant from doing more than urging the police to enter.

Perhaps the most serious consequence of the majority's rule is its operation in domestic abuse situations, a context in which the present question often arises.... While people living together might typically be accommodating to the wishes of their cotenants, requests for police assistance may well come from coinhabitants who are having a disagreement. The Court concludes that because "no sensible person would go inside" in the face of disputed consent, ... and the consenting cotenant thus has "no recognized authority" to insist on the guest's admission, ... a "police officer [has] no better claim to reasonableness in entering than the officer would have in the absence of any consent at all...." But the police officer's superior claim to enter is obvious: Mrs. Randolph did not invite the police to join her for dessert and coffee; the officer's precise purpose in knocking on the door was to assist with a dispute between the Randolphs--one in which Mrs. Randolph felt the need for the protective presence of the police. The majority's rule apparently forbids police from entering to assist with a domestic dispute if the abuser whose behavior prompted the request for police assistance objects.[144]

"One element that can make a warrantless government search of a home '"reasonable"' is voluntary consent .... Proof of voluntary consent "is not limited to proof that consent was given by the defendant," but the government "may show that permission to search was obtained from a third party who possessed common authority over or other sufficient relationship to the premises."[145] Thus, according to the dissenting Justices' reading of Court precedent, co-occupants have "'assumed the risk that one of their number might permit [a] common area to be searched.' Just as Mrs. Randolph could walk upstairs, come down, and turn her husband's cocaine straw over to the police, she can consent to police entry and search of what is, after all, her home, too."[146]

Notes and Questions

1.   What type of data source does the majority rely on to justify its interpretation of the Fourth Amendment?

2.   Is the majority right to rely on social expectations in the consent context rather than in the reasonable expectations of privacy for a search context? Do you agree that social expectations are as the majority describes them?

3.   Is the dissent's reliance on assumption of risk a normative judgment or an alternative analysis of social expectations?

4.   Do you agree with the dissent that the majority's approach

---

[144] *Id.* at 1537-38 (Roberts, Chief J., dissenting).

[145] *Id.* at 1532 (Roberts, Chief J., dissenting, citing *Matlock)*.

[146] *Id.* at 1531 (Roberts, Chief J., dissenting).

will leave domestic abuse victims at the mercy of their abusers? What if the *Randolph* facts differed in this one respect: Mrs. Randolph's complaint was that her husband had just been beating her, that there was a bloody dress in the bedroom to prove it, and that she feared that he was about to beat her again. How would the majority's rule approach this situation?

Page 432, footnote 13. Insert the following at the end of the footnote:

For those interested in a far more detailed revisionist history of the Fourth Amendment and its modern implications, *see* ANDREW E. TASLITZ, RECONSTRUCTING THE FOURTH AMENDMENT: A HISTORY OF SEARCH AND SEIZURE, 1789-1868 (forthcoming N.Y.U. Press October 1, 2006).

Page 452. Insert the following immediately after Question 3 and before Problem 5-3:

4. Would it matter if the prosecutor and the defendant shared the same race? For a discussion of the ethical obligations of a Black prosecutor in the American criminal justice system, see Lenese Herbert, *"Et in Arcadia Ego: A Perspective On Black Prosecutors' Loyalty Within the American Criminal Justice System,"* ___ Howard L.J. ___ (forthcoming 2006).

CHAPTER 6

SEARCHES AND SEIZURES: TERRORISM, SURVEILLANCE, AND SPECIAL STATUTORY POWERS

III. STATUTORY REGULATION OF SURVEILLANCE

C. THE USA PATRIOT ACT

Page 511. Delete heading 2, "Potential Additions to the Patriot Act," and everything under it through page 512, replacing that material with the following:

2. REAUTHORIZATION AND MODIFICATION OF THE PATRIOT ACT

In March 2006, the President signed a bill reauthorizing the Patriot Act. The substance of most of its surveillance provisions remained largely intact. The following modifications are, however, worth noting here:

a. Section 215 had previously authorized the FBI to order any person or entity to turn over "any tangible things" so long as the FBI "specif[ies]" that the order is "for an authorized investigation...to protect against international terrorism or clandestine intelligence activities." Neither probable cause nor reasonable suspicion of crime nor that the investigation was of a foreign power or its agent were required. Section 215 survives substantially in its original form, but businesses have an express right to challenge records orders under that section.

b. National Security Letters issued by the FBI for financial records and internet or phone number logs without a court order are now strengthened, becoming National Security Subpoenas, subjecting non-complying businesses to being held in contempt by courts. Any employee intentionally disclosing a demand for these records can be imprisoned for five years unless the subpoena or the gag order have first been successfully challenged in court.

c. Businesses that receive an order for records of employees or customers now have an express right to consult an attorney, including about whether to challenge the order.

d. Gag orders are not automatic and need not be permanent restrictions on free speech, but customers or employees whose personal records are demanded cannot be told that their records were turned over to the government unless the accompanying gag order has been discontinued. If a high-level political appointee certifies that national security or diplomatic relations will be harmed, the court must consider that assertion conclusive – unless made in "bad faith" – thus ensuring that the gag order will stand.

e. Sneak and peek warrants initially will include a seven day delay in notice, subject to extensions and exceptions. But these warrants can be obtained even in cases that have nothing to do with terrorism.

f. Domestic terrorism has been re-defined more narrowly than before so that it is now limited to specific federal terrorism crimes.

g. A new four-year sunset date has been placed on three provisions:

(i) Section 215 (discussed above; often called the "library provision," though its reach is broader);

(ii) Section 206, permitting roving wiretaps; and

(iii) the so-called "lone wolf provision," added by the 2004 intelligence bill, which applies FISA secret surveillance procedures to non-US citizens in this country without requiring that they be acting for a foreign power.[147]

Page 515. Insert the following after the sentence supported by footnote 20:

The following is a recent example of the government's post-September 11th use of the material witness warrant: in May, 2004, the FBI arrested Portland, Oregon lawyer Brandon Mayfield as a material witness in the Madrid, Spain train station bombing. Mayfield was held for two weeks before the government acknowledged that a fingerprint it had thought was his in fact belonged to someone else. A reporter for the Portland Oregonian, analyzing Mayfield's situation, reported that "[t]he Justice Department reported to Congress that as of January 2003, nearly 50 people had been detained as material witnesses in connection with the investigation of the Sept. 11 attacks. Since then, however, it has refused to update the statistics, saying they are covered by grand jury secrecy rules."[148]

---

[147] American Civil Liberties Union, *The Patriot Act: Where It Stands*, http://action.aclu.org/reformthepatriiotact/whereitstands.html.

[148] Mark Larabee, *Portland Case Fuels Rights Debate*, THE OREGONIAN (May 31, 2004).

The Mayfield case prompted this editorial from The Washington Post[149]:

When Portland, Ore., lawyer Brandon Mayfield was taken into federal custody two weeks ago under a material-witness warrant, an indictment seemed likely to follow. A fingerprint belonging to Mayfield, who had converted to Islam, reportedly had been found on a bag of detonators connected to the deadly Madrid bombing, and Mr. Mayfield had done legal work for an Islamic radical successfully prosecuted in Oregon. Yet this week Mr. Mayfield walked out of detention a free man; Spanish police had reportedly tied the fingerprint on the bag to an Algerian. And the Justice Department now finds itself with some explaining to do.

A gag order on the case makes information scant, and the court, in releasing him, noted that his "release will be supervised" and that there will be "further grand jury proceedings wherein he remains a material witness." Many more facts may yet emerge. It isn't too soon, however, to ask whether someone misread a fingerprint, and if so who and why; or to worry that federal authorities might have arrested someone without the evidence to bring a responsible case.

The case is the latest example of the Justice Department's aggressive use of the power to detain "material witnesses" -- people with evidence in a court proceeding who might flee if left at large. The statute, which authorizes such detentions under court supervision for "a reasonable period of time" in order to secure testimony, is not new. It has long been used with relatively little controversy in organized-crime cases.

---

[149] *Arresting Witnesses*, THE WASHINGTON POST (Editorial, May 22, 2004).

But since the Oklahoma City bombing investigation and particularly since Sept. 11, 2001, designation of material witnesses has become a more routine tool in the government's legal arsenal and has been deployed at an earlier stage of criminal proceedings. Rather than being used merely to ensure that witnesses are available for trial after an indictment has been issued, it has been employed to hold suspects who are themselves under investigation. The result is that dozens of people across the country have been detained for varying periods of time while the government seeks to compile evidence against them. The circumstances of these detentions are shrouded in secrecy, as are the names of the detainees and even the raw number of them. The Justice Department at times has seemed to use the statute as a kind of preventive detention law.

Congress, which has shown little interest in legislating on difficult matters involving liberty and security, has failed to clarify the new circumstances under which the material-witness law should apply. The result is a detention authority for which the parameters are dangerously undefined. How long is a "reasonable period of time" for the government to hold someone without charge while digging around to see if it can make a case? In typical criminal cases, the government is required to bring charges in order to hold any suspect. If that is to change in terrorism cases, the change should come as a result of a deliberate legislative decision, not the mission creep of an old statute envisioned for other problems.

Even if Mr. Mayfield's case does not prove to be an example of an abuse of the power, the use of the material-witness law needs careful attention and a healthy dose of sunlight.

Page 521. Insert the following after the first sentence in Note 1:

On appeal, Judge Kessler's order in *Center for National Security Studies* was reversed.[150] Writing for a 2-judge majority, Judge David Sentelle stated:

> The government invokes four exemptions— 7(A), 7(C), 7(F), and 3—to shield the names of detainees from disclosure. Upon review, we hold that Exemption 7(A) was properly invoked to withhold the names of the detainees and their lawyers. Finding the names protected under 7(A), we need not address the other exemptions invoked by the government and reserve judgment on whether they too would support withholding the names.
>
> Exemption 7(A) allows an agency to withhold "records or information compiled for law enforcement purposes, but only to the extent that the production of such law enforcement records or information ... could reasonably be expected to interfere with enforcement proceedings." ...
>
> ... [P]laintiffs urge that Exemption 7(A) does not apply because disclosure is not "reasonably likely to interfere with enforcement proceedings." We disagree. Under Exemption 7(A), the government has the burden of demonstrating a reasonable likelihood of interference .... The government's declarations, viewed in light of the appropriate deference to the executive on issues of national security, satisfy this burden. ...
>
> For several reasons, plaintiffs contend that we should reject the government's predictive judgments of the harms that would result from

---

[150] 331 F.3d 918 (D.C. Cir. 2003), *cert. denied*, 540 U.S. 1104 (2004).

disclosure. First, they argue that terrorist organizations likely already know which of their members have been detained. We have no way of assessing that likelihood. Moreover, even if terrorist organizations know about some of their members who were detained, a complete list of detainees could still have great value in confirming the status of their members. For example, an organization may be unaware of a member who was detained briefly and then released, but remains subject to continuing government surveillance. After disclosure, this detainee could be irreparably compromised as a source of information.

More importantly, some detainees may not be members of terrorist organizations, but may nonetheless have been detained on INS or material witness warrants as having information about terrorists. Terrorist organizations are less likely to be aware of such individuals' status as detainees. Such detainees could be acquaintances of the September 11 terrorists, or members of the same community groups or mosques. *See* Rachel L. Swarns, *Oregon Muslims Protest Monthlong Detention Without a Charge,* N.Y. TIMES, April 20, 2003, at A16 (describing material witness detainee who attended same mosque as indicted terrorism suspects). These detainees, fearing retribution or stigma, would be less likely to cooperate with the investigation if their names are disclosed. Moreover, tracking down the background and location of these detainees could give terrorists insights into the investigation they would otherwise be unlikely to have. After disclosure, terrorist organizations could attempt to intimidate these detainees or their families, or feed the detainees false or misleading information. It is important to remember that many of these detainees have been released at this time and are thus especially vulnerable to intimidation or coercion. While the detainees have been free to disclose their names to the press or public, it is telling that so few have come forward, perhaps for fear of this very intimidation.

We further note the impact disclosure could have on the government's investigation going forward. A potential witness or informant may be much less likely to come forward and cooperate with the investigation if he believes his name will be made public. ...

Contrary to plaintiffs' claims, the government's submissions easily establish an adequate connection between both the material witness and the INS detainees and terrorism to warrant full application of the deference principle. First, all material witness detainees have been held on warrants issued by a federal judge pursuant to 18 U.S.C. § 3144. Under this statute, a federal judge may issue a material witness warrant based on an affidavit stating that the witness has information relevant to an ongoing criminal investigation. Consequently, material witness detainees have been found by a federal judge to have relevant knowledge about the terrorism investigation. It is therefore reasonable to assume that disclosure of their names could impede the government's use of these potentially valuable witnesses. ...

In upholding the government's invocation of Exemption 7(A), we observe that we are in accord with several federal courts that have wisely respected the executive's judgment in prosecuting the national response to terrorism. *See Hamdi v. Rumsfeld,* 316 F.3d 450 (4th Cir.2003) (dismissing the *habeas corpus* petition of a United States citizen captured in Afghanistan challenging his military detention and designation as an enemy combatant); *Hamdi v. Rumsfeld,* 296 F.3d 278 (4th Cir.2002) (reversing district court's order that allowed alleged enemy combatant unmonitored access to counsel). We realize that not all courts are in agreement. In *Detroit Free Press v. Ashcroft*, 303 F.3d 681 (6th Cir.2002), the Sixth Circuit acknowledged the necessity of deferring to the executive on terrorism issues but held that the First Amendment prohibits a blanket closure of "special interest deportation hearings." We do not find the Sixth Circuit's reasoning compelling, but join the Third, Fourth, and Seventh Circuits in holding that the courts must defer to the executive on decisions of national security. In so deferring, we do not abdicate the role of the judiciary. Rather, in undertaking a deferential review we simply recognize the different roles underlying the constitutional separation of powers. It is within the role of the executive to acquire and exercise the expertise of protecting national security. It is not within the role of the courts to second-guess executive judgments made in furtherance of that branch's proper role. The judgment of the district court ordering the government to disclose the names of the detainees is reversed.

Consider: in the following materials, we describe the Supreme Court's treatment of the *Hamdi* case. In light of the fact that the majority in *Center for National Security Studies* relied on the lower court opinions in *Hamdi*, do you think the majority's decision is still sound?

Page 522. Insert the following after the discussion of *Hamdi v. Rumsfeld* to complete Section G (and conclude Chapter Six):

G. EXTENDED DETENTION OF PERSONS IN THE WAR ON TERRORISM

In addition to detaining persons pursuant to material witness warrants, the United States has engaged in extended detentions of individuals in the War on Terrorism on a variety of other grounds.[151] Although the United States Supreme Court has chosen not to rest its very recent and few decisions in this area on Fourth Amendment grounds, it has recognized important due process and related protection for these detainees that merit at least brief mention in this Supplement. These cases also matter because at least one of them recognizes the importance of the right to counsel in preventing governmental excess in a perhaps indefinite war.

Hamdi v. Rumsfeld[152] raised the question whether Yaser Hamdi, an American citizen captured in a combat zone in Afghanistan, then taken to the U.S. naval base at Guantanamo Bay, Cuba, and finally jailed in a naval brig on the east coast of the United States, could be held indefinitely without serious judicial review, in solitary confinement, with no visitors and no access to lawyers, because he was designated by the Executive as an "enemy combatant." The Court, in a fractured set of opinions, answered this question with a resounding "no."

Hamdi's father had filed a habeas corpus petition on Hamdi's behalf. The Justice Department sought summary dismissal on the ground that the court could not "second guess" the Executive's "enemy combatant" designation. The Fourth Circuit ultimately dismissed the petition, finding that Hamdi's own legal papers conceded that Hamdi was seized in a zone of overseas combat and that that was sufficient to justify deference to the

---

[151] *See generally* Barbara Olshansky, AMERICA'S DISAPPEARED: SECRET IMPRISONMENT, DETAINEES, AND THE WAR ON TERROR (2004).
[152] 542 U.S. 507 (2004).

President's decision.

In the United States Supreme Court, only Justice Thomas agreed with the Government's position. The plurality opinion, signed on to by Justices O'Connor, Rehnquist, Kennedy, and Breyer, held that "due process demands that a citizen held in the United States as an enemy combatant be given a meaningful opportunity to contest the factual basis for that detention before a neutral decisionmaker. ... Plainly, the 'process' Hamdi has received is not that to which he is entitled under the Due Process Clause."[153] The plurality thus not only rejected the Government's claim that the judiciary owed virtually unquestioned deference to the Executive on this matter, but also rejected the Government's fallback position that production of but "some evidence" from the Department of Defense demonstrating that the detention was not wholly arbitrary—a burden met by the affidavit of a Pentagon official—was adequate to support the President's decision.[154] The plurality likewise rejected the Government's blockade of Hamdi's access to counsel, unequivocally declaring that Hamdi "unquestionably has the right to access to counsel."[155] The Court remanded the case to the Fourth Circuit for further proceedings in which Hamdi will have the opportunity to show that the Executive's enemy designation was wrong.

Justice Scalia, in an opinion joined by Justice Stevens, would have gone further, issuing the writ of habeas corpus and discharging Hamdi without remanding the case for unnecessary further proceedings. Justice Scalia read the history of habeas corpus as demonstrating that the Great Writ could be suspended only by congressional, not executive, action while the courts were open and that "Citizens aiding the enemy have been treated as traitors subject to criminal process."[156] Furthermore, said Justice Scalia, the Non-Detention Act was intended to prohibit precisely such executive detentions. That Act, passed by Congress in 1971 to prevent the recurrence of events like the Japanese-American internment camps during World War II, declared that "[n]o citizen

---

[153] *Id.* at 509, 538 (O'Connor, J., plurality opinion).

[154] *See id.* at 537-39 (O'Connor, J., plurality opinion).

[155] *Id.* at 539 (O'Connor, J., plurality opinion).

[156] *Id.* at 559 (Scalia, J., dissenting).

shall be imprisoned or otherwise detained by the United States except pursuant to an Act of Congress."[157] Justice Scalia rejected the argument, articulated in the plurality opinion, that the Authorization for Use of Military Force Act (authorizing the President to use "all necessary and appropriate force against nations, organizations, or persons he determines planned, authorized, committed, or aided the terrorist attacks that occurred on September 11, 2001 … to prevent any future acts of international terrorism against the United States"[158]) constituted adequate congressional action because detention is a "necessary and appropriate" use of force.[159] Justice Scalia did "not think this statute even authorizes detention of a citizen with the clarity necessary to satisfy the interpretive canon that statutes should be construed so as to avoid grave constitutional concerns."[160] Moreover, he said, the statute was "not remotely a congressional suspension of the writ, and no one claims that it is."[161] Therefore, in the view of Justices Scalia and Stevens, the Government had only two choices absent clear congressional action suspending the writ of habeas corpus: release Hamdi or process him through the ordinary criminal justice system.

Justices Souter and Ginsburg likewise agreed that remand was unnecessary because the Non-Detention Act barred detention of citizens on United States soil without explicit congressional authorization. Justice Souter explained:

> The fact that Congress intended to guard against a repetition of the World War II internments when it repealed the 1950 [Cold War statute authorizing the Attorney General in time of emergency to detain anyone reasonably thought likely to engage in sabotage or espionage] and gave us §4001(a) provides a powerful reason to think that §4001(a) was meant to require clear congressional authorization before any citizen can be placed in a

---

[157] 18 U.S.C. §4001(a).

[158] 115 Stat. 224.

[159] *Hamdi*, 542 U.S. at 575 n.5 (Scalia, J., dissenting).

[160] *Id.* at 574 (Scalia, J., dissenting).

[161] *Id.* (Scalia, J., dissenting).

cell. It is not merely that the legislative history shows that §4001(a) was thought necessary in anticipation of times just like the present, in which the safety of the country is threatened. To appreciate what is most significant, one must recall that the internments of the 1940s were accomplished by Executive action. Although an Act of Congress ratified and confirmed an Executive order authorizing the military to exclude individuals from defined areas and to accommodate those it might remove, ... the statute said nothing whatever about the detention of those who might be removed, ...; internment camps were creatures of the Executive, and confinement in them rested on assertion of Executive authority.... When, therefore, Congress repealed the 1950 Act and adopted §4001(a) for the purpose of avoiding another *Korematsu*, it intended to preclude reliance on vague congressional authority (for example, providing "accommodations" for those subject to removal) as authority for detention or imprisonment at the discretion of the Executive (maintaining detention camps of American citizens, for example). In requiring that any Executive detention be "pursuant to an Act of Congress," then, Congress necessarily meant to require a congressional enactment that clearly authorized detention or imprisonment. ...

Under this principle of reading §4001(a) robustly to require a clear statement of authorization to detain, none of the Government's arguments suffices to justify Hamdi's detention.[162]

Nevertheless, Justices Souter and Ginsburg joined in the plurality's remand "to give practical effect to the conclusions of eight members of the Court [in] rejecting the Government's position."[163]

---

[162] *Id.* at 544-45 (Souter, J., concurring in part, dissenting in part, concurring in the judgment).

[163] *Id.* at 553 (Souter, J., concurring in part, dissenting in part, concurring in the

Despite the majority signing onto a remand, however, there were important limitations on the plurality's opinion. First, a clear majority (Chief Justice Rehnquist and Justices O'Connor, Breyer, Kennedy, and Thomas) explicitly recognized the President's authority to designate both citizens and non-citizens as enemy combatants and, though less clear on the point, should the War on Terrorism prove to be a conflict of near-indefinite duration, this same majority arguably agreed for now that such individuals can be held in custody without criminal charge or trial for the entire duration of the conflict.[164] Second, five Justices also concluded that the Authorization for Use of Military Force Act overcame any objection that the detention of American citizens violated the Non-Detention Act. Third, the plurality's opinion and at least that of Justice Scalia and Stevens were limited to "*citizen*-detainees."

Fourth, although the citizen-detainee can turn to the courts or to other sorts of tribunals to challenge an enemy-combatant designation, the process due is limited. Said the plurality, that process must include the detainee's receiving "notice of the factual basis for his classification, and a fair opportunity to rebut the government's factual assertions before a neutral decisionmaker."[165] However, the plurality suggested that the "standards we have articulated could be met by an appropriately authorized and constituted military tribunal" like the Article V tribunals already governed by Army regulation where the Geneva Convention applies.[166] Article III courts might, therefore, not necessarily be involved. Further, the burden can be shifted to the detainee to prove that he is *not* an enemy combatant once the Government "puts forth credible evidence that the habeas petitioner meets the enemy combatant criteria," a standard highly deferential to the Government.[167] Explained the plurality, such burden-shifting

---

judgment).

[164] *Cf.* Timothy Lynch, *No Blank Check*, pamphlet published by The Federalist Society for Law and Policy Studies (July 2004) (counting votes and reaching similar conclusion); Lee A. Casey, David B. Rivkin, Jr., and Darin R. Bartram, *The Supreme Court's 2004 "War on Terror" Cases*, pamphlet published by The Federalist Society for Law and Policy Studies (July 2004) (similar).

[165] *Hamdi*, 542 U.S. at 533 (O'Connor, J., plurality opinion).

[166] *Id.* at 538 (O'Connor, J., plurality opinion).

[167] *Id.* at 534 (O'Connor, J., plurality opinion).

would still "meet the goal of ensuring that the errant tourist, embedded journalist, or local aid worker has a chance to prove military error while giving due regard to the Executive once it has put forth meaningful support for its conclusion that the detainee is in fact an enemy combatant."[168] However, the plurality and at least three other Justices (the total lineup including Justices O'Connor, Kennedy, Breyer, Souter, Ginsburg, and Chief Justice Rehnquist) insisted that the detainees would be entitled to the assistance of counsel, offering no clear rationale, perhaps on the apparent assumption that the centrality of counsel to due process was self-evident.[169]

Rumsfeld v. Padilla[170] had in some ways been the most eagerly anticipated of the Court's opinions on detention of suspected terrorists because it involved an American citizen initially detained on United States soil. Padilla was allegedly trained abroad by Al Qaeda, re-entering the U.S. with the goal of detonating a radiological "dirty" bomb. He was taken into custody at Chicago's O'Hare International Airport, and then transferred to New York City on the basis of a material witness warrant, where he was assigned counsel. He was, however, transferred to military custody, now being held at the Naval Brig at Charleston, South Carolina, when, only a few days after being assigned counsel, his status was re-designated by the President as an enemy combatant.

When Padilla's lawyer filed a habeas petition in the Southern District of New York, the District Court rejected the Government's claim that Padilla was not entitled to counsel but held that the President had authority to designate Padilla an enemy combatant, a decision entitled to substantial deference by the judiciary. The Second Circuit reversed, concluding that, as an American citizen, Padilla could not be held as an enemy combatant but must be released or be processed through the regular criminal justice system. The Second Circuit relied on a reading of the Non-Detention Act, similar to that later articulated by Justice Scalia in *Hamdi*, forbidding prolonged detention of American citizens absent contrary congressional enactment.

---

[168] *Id.* (O'Connor, J., plurality opinion).
[169] *See* Lynch, *supra* note 164; Casey, et al., *supra* note 164.
[170] 542 U.S. 426 (2004).

However, the high Court disappointed observers by not resolving the substantive issue, instead ruling that the petition had been filed in the wrong court and needed to be re-filed in the District of South Carolina, where Padilla's "immediate custodian" held Padilla in detention. Justice Stevens, joined by Justices Souter, Ginsburg, and Breyer, dissented, arguing that the case's merits should have been addressed because of their "profound importance."[171] Given the Court's decision on *Hamdi*, however, when Padilla re-files, he will likely be accorded access to present his case to a "neutral decisionmaker."[172]

Finally, *Rasul v. Bush*[173] involved *non*-citizen detainees at the United States Naval Station, Guantanamo Bay, Cuba ("Gitmo"), purportedly beyond U.S. territory because of Cuba's retention over Guantanamo's "ultimate sovereignty" when leasing the area to the U.S. in 1903. The Government had argued that the courts lacked habeas jurisdiction over non-citizen detainees held outside United States territory, relying on *Johnson v. Eisentrager*,[174] in which the Court rejected petitions by German nationals captured in China at the end of World War II and held under American authority in post-war Germany because those claimants were outside U.S. territory and thus beyond the federal court's jurisdiction. The United States Court of Appeals for the District of Columbia Circuit agreed with the Government's position that *Eisentrager* controlled in *Rasul* and that the Gitmo detainees could not challenge their detention.

The Court reversed in a 5-4 split, with the majority's opinion authored by Justice Stevens and joined by Justices O'Connor, Souter, Ginsburg, and Breyer, with Justice Kennedy concurring in the result. Justice Stevens found no inherent constitutional right to habeas review beyond U.S. territory, at least for aliens. However, he distinguished *Eisentrager* on the ground that the Court had there *assumed* that statutory habeas review was unavailable. But, said Justice Stevens, subsequent Supreme Court

---

[171] *Id.* at 2730 (Stevens, J., dissenting).

[172] *See* Lynch, *supra* note 164; Casey, et al., *supra* note 164.

[173] 542 U.S. 466 (2004).

[174] 339 U.S. 763 (1950).

decisions clarified that even non-citizens held overseas can obtain review under the habeas corpus statute, 28 U.S. C. §2241. Accordingly, the Gitmo detainees could challenge the legality of their detention via the federal habeas process. Given the statutory basis of the majority's decision, however, Congress may remain free to amend the habeas statute to alter this result.[175] And given *Hamdi's* decision on the limited due process rights of citizen-detainees, it is also unlikely that the aliens in the *Rasul* case will be accorded any greater process.[176]

Justice Scalia, joined by Chief Justice Rehnquist and Justice Thomas, dissented on a number of grounds, including that the majority misread *Eisentrager* and effectively extended the habeas statute "to the four corners of the earth."[177]

Military commissions, tribunals "neither mentioned in the Constitution nor created by statute [were] born of military necessity." [178]   Over a half-century ago, the Supreme Court recognized that trial by military commission "'is an extraordinary measure raising important questions about the balance of powers in our constitutional structure.'" [179]   That message bore reiteration most recently in *Hamdan v. Rumsfeld*.[180] In *Hamdan*, petitioner, Salim Ahmed Hamdan, a Yemeni national, was captured and turned over to the U.S. military during the invasion of Afghanistan pursuant to Congress's adoption of legislation that authorized the president, George W. Bush, to

> [u]se all necessary and appropriate force against those nations, organizations, or persons he determines planned, authorized, committed, or aided the terrorist attacks ... in order to prevent any future acts of international terrorism against the

---

[175] *See* Lynch, *supra* note 164 Casey, et al., *supra* note 164.

[176] *See* Casey, *supra*.

[177] *Id.* at 2706 (Scalia, J., dissenting).

[178] *Hamdan v. Rumsfeld*, 2006 U.S. LEXIS 5185 at *60 (June 29, 2006).

[179] *Id* (<u>citing</u> *Ex parte Quirin*, 317 U.S. 1, 19 (1942)).

[180] *Id.*

United States by such nations, organizations, or persons. [181]

The joint resolution was enacted shortly after the September 11, 2001, al Qaeda terror attacks on the World Trade Center and the Pentagon. As a result of the joint resolution, hundreds of individuals, including Hamdan, were captured and transported as detainees/prisoners in Guantánamo Bay, Cuba. On November 13, 2001, President Bush issued a military order which vested in the Secretary of Defense the power to appoint military commissions to try individuals subject to the order, which also governed how non-American detainees in the so-called "War Against Terrorism" would be treated. Hamdan, deemed by the President of the United States to be eligible for trial by military commission, was regarded as an "enemy combatant," *i.e.,* "part of or supporting Taliban or al Qaeda forces, or associated forces that are engaged in hostilities against the United States or its coalition partners." [182] Ultimately, Hamdan was charged with conspiracy "to commit ... offenses triable by military commission" that spanned 1996 to November 2001.

Hamdan asserted that the military commission lacked authority to try him because: (1) neither congressional Act nor the common law of war supports trial by this commission for conspiracy, an offense that, Hamdan says, is not a violation of the law of war; and (2) the procedures adopted to try him violate basic tenets of military and international law, including but not limited to, the principle that a defendant must be permitted to see and hear the evidence against him. Attorneys for the Bush administration argued the contrary, asserting further that Hamdan and other Guantánamo detainees were not covered by the Geneva Conventions on treatment of prisoners of war.

The Supreme Court, in a 5-to-3 decision, agreed with Hamdan. Justice Stevens, writing for the majority, determined that the commission convened to try Hamdan lacks power to proceed

---

[181] *Id.* at *22 (quoting Authorization for Use of Military Force, 115 Stat. 224, note following 50 U.S.C. §1541 (2000 ed., Supp. III)).
[182] *Id.* at *27 n.1.

because its structure and procedures violate both the Uniform Code of Military Justice and the Geneva Conventions:

> [t]he charge against Hamdan ... alleges a conspiracy extending over a number of years, from 1996 to November 2001. all but two months of that more than 5-year-long period preceded the attacks of September 11, 2001, and the enactment of the AUMF -- the Act of Congress on which the Government relies for exercise of its war powers and thus for its authority to convene military commissions. Neither the purported agreement with Osama bin Laden and others to commit war crimes, nor a single overt act, is alleged to have occurred in a theater of war or on any specified date after September 11, 2001. None of the overt acts that Hamdan is alleged to have committed violates the law of war. .. . . the offense alleged must have been committed both in a theater of war and *during*, not before the relevant conflict.... [t]he deficiencies in the time and place allegations also underscore – indeed are symptomatic of – the most serious defect of this charge: The offense it alleges is not triable by law-of-war military commission.

> ...

> At a minimum, the Government must make a substantial showing that the crime for which it seeks to try a defendant by military commission is acknowledged to be an offense against the law of war. That burden is far from satisfied here. The crime of conspiracy has rarely if ever been tried as such in this country by any law-of-war military commission not exercising some other form of jurisdiction, and does not appear in either the Geneva Conventions or the Hague Conventions – the major treaties on the law of war.[183]

---

[183] *Id.* at *75-77, 80-81.

As a result of the Court's decision, lawyers for other Guantánamo detainees are considering whether to file habeas corpus petitions to challenge their detentions. These and other lawyers may also use *Hamdan* to challenge detentions at other locations worldwide that house "high value" U.S.-held detainees (including senior al Qaeda officials) in secret jails run by the U.S. Central Intelligence Agency.[184] As for the governmental response, President Bush could request specific, *Hamdan*-responsive legislation that would allow his administration to create a detainee-specific criminal justice system that would conform with the Court's ruling.[185]

---

[184] *See* Neil A. Lewis, "Detainees May Test Reach of Guantánamo Ruling," New York Times (July 1, 2006), located at http://www.nytimes.com/2006/07/01/us/01geneva.html?_r=1&n=Top%2fReference%2fTimes%20Topics%2fOrganizations%2fS%2fSupreme%20Court%20&oref=slogin .

[185] *See* Linda Greenhouse, "Justices, 5-3, Broadly Reject Bush Plan to Try Detainees," New York Times, Section A1 (June 30, 2006), located at http://www.nytimes.com/2006/06/30/washington/30hamdan.html?n=Top%2fReference%2fTimes%20Topics%2fOrganizations%2fS%2fSupreme%20Court%20

CHAPTER 7

SEARCHES AND SEIZURES: THE EXCLUSIONARY RULE

II. LIMITATIONS ON EXCLUDING FRUITS OF THE POISONOUS TREE

C. ATTENUATION OF THE TAINT

Pages 537-43. Delete the *Brown v. Illinois* excerpt at these pages and substitute the Notes and Questions at Pages 543-45 and the inserts on *Kaupp v. Texas* and *Hudson v. Michigan* below in this Supplement.

Page 544. Insert the following just before the last *full* paragraph, which begins with the sentence "Consent searches frequently raise attenuation issues":

The Court recently applied the *Brown* factors to determine whether to suppress a confession resulting from an arrest of a juvenile without probable cause in *Kaupp v. Texas*.[186] The police brought the 19-year-old half brother of a 14-year-old missing girl in for questioning. They also brought Kaupp to the police station for the same purpose because he had been in the *half-brother's* company on the date of the disappearance. Kaupp was cooperative and permitted to leave, but the half-brother thrice failed a polygraph test, eventually admitting that he had stabbed his half sister and placed her body in a drainage ditch. The half-brother also implicated Kaupp in the crime.

Detectives immediately tried, but failed, to obtain a warrant

---

[186] 538 U.S. 626 (2003).

to question Kaupp. Detective Pinkins, hoping to confront Kaupp with the half-brother's statement, and accompanied by two other plain clothes detectives and three uniformed officers, went to Kaupp's house and were admitted by his father a 3 a.m. on a January morning. Pinkins, with at least two other officers, awakened Kaupp in his bedroom by shining a flashlight, identified himself, and said, "'[W]e need to go and talk.'" Kaupp said "'Okay,'" and two officers handcuffed him, leading him shoeless and still in boxer shorts and a T-shirt, to a police car. The car stopped for 5 or 10 minutes where the victim's body had been found, then continued on to the sheriff's headquarters. There, police placed Kaupp in an interview room, removed his handcuffs, and *Mirandized* him.

Although he initially denied any involvement in the crime, within 10 or 15 minutes of interrogation, and after being confronted with the half-brother's confession, Kaupp admitted having some part in the crime, without confessing to the murder itself or acknowledging causing the fatal wound. He was subsequently indicted and convicted of murder, having lost his motion to suppress his statements as fruits of an illegal arrest. Texas appellate courts affirmed the conviction, concluding that no arrest had yet taken place, thus no probable cause was required.

When the case reached the Supreme Court, the state conceded that the detectives lacked probable cause. But they argued that Kaupp voluntarily consented to accompany the officers to the station for questioning and that, therefore, no "arrest" had been made by the time of questioning. The Court rejected these claims without dissent. However, though expressing doubt that the state could succeed in avoiding suppression of Kaupp's confession, the Court remanded the case to the trial court to determine whether Kaupp's statements fit within *Brown's* attenuation exception to the exclusionary rule. The Court reasoned thus:

> Since Kaupp was arrested before he was questioned, and because the state does not even claim that the sheriff's department had probable cause to detain him at that point, well-established precedent requires suppression of the confession

unless that confession was "an act of free will [sufficient] to purge the primary taint of the unlawful invasion." Demonstrating such purgation is, of course, a function of circumstantial evidence, with the burden of persuasion on the state. Relevant considerations include observation of *Miranda,* "[t]he temporal proximity of the arrest and the confession, the presence of intervening circumstances, and, particularly, the purpose and flagrancy of the official misconduct....

The record before us shows that only one of these considerations, the giving of *Miranda* warnings, supports the state, and we held in *Brown* that "*Miranda* warnings, *alone* and *per se*, cannot always ... break, for Fourth Amendment purposes, the casual connection between the illegality and the confession.... All other factors point the opposite way. There is no indication from the record that any substantial time passed between Kaupp's removal from his home in handcuffs and his confession after only 10 or 15 minutes of interrogation. In the interview, he remained in his partially clothed state in the physical custody of a number of officers, some of whom, at least, were conscious that they lacked probable cause to arrest. In fact, the state has not even alleged "any meaningful intervening event" between the illegal arrest and Kaupp's confession. Unless, on remand, the state can point to testimony undisclosed on the record before us and weighty enough to carry the State's burden despite the clear force of the evidence shown here, the confession must be suppressed.[187]

---

[187] *Id.* at 633.

Page 545. Insert the following just before the heading, "Fruit of the Poisonous Tree Problems."

Recently, the Court gave a new spin to the attenuation doctrine as well as to the independent source doctrine in *Booker T. Hudson, Jr. v. Michigan*,[188] which addressed the propriety of suppression as a remedy for "knock-and-announce" violations. There, Detroit, Michigan police obtained and executed a search warrant for drugs and firearms in Hudson's home in violation of the Fourth Amendment's "knock-and-announce" rule (when they arrived to execute the warrant, they announced their presence and waited "three to five seconds" before turning the unlocked front door knob and entering Hudson's home). Hudson moved to suppress all inculpatory evidence seized, arguing that the "premature entry" violated his Fourth Amendment right against unreasonable search and seizure.

The Supreme Court determined that violation of the knock-and-announce rule does not require as a remedy suppression of the seized evidence. Even if there were a "but-for" connection between the violation and the discovery of the evidence, said the Court, attenuation occurs in two circumstances: first, when the causal connection is remote; second, when the *specific interests* protected by the particular constitutional guarantee violated would not be served by suppression. (The Court argued that both sorts of attenuation were rooted in precedent, but this second sort had not been so clearly identified before as a distinct form of attenuation). Three specific interests were protected by the knock-and-announce rule, in the Court's view: (1) the protection of life and limb "because an unannounced entry may provoke violence in supposed self-defense by the surprised resident."; (2) the protection of property because individuals have the opportunity to comply with the law rather than suffer forcible damage to their dwelling; and (3) "those elements of privacy and dignity that can be destroyed by a sudden entrance," in short, "assur[ing] the opportunity to collect oneself before answering the door." Concluded the Court:

---

[188] 547 U.S. __ (2006)(slip op.).

What the knock-and-announce rule has never protected, however, is one's interest in preventing the government from seeing or taking evidence described in a warrant. Since the interests that *were* violated in this case have nothing to do with the seizure of the evidence, the exclusionary rule is inapplicable.[189]

The Court continued, however, declaring: "Quite apart from the requirements of unattenuated causation, the exclusionary rule has never been applied except 'where its deterrence benefits outweigh its substantial social costs.'" Accordingly, the remedy "has always been our last resort, not our first impulse.". Concerning the knock-and-announce rule violation, the Court found the costs of suppression to be considerable:

> In addition to the grave adverse consequence that exclusion of relevant incriminating evidence always entails (viz., the risk of releasing dangerous criminals into society), imposing that massive remedy for a knock-and-announce violation would generate a constant flood of alleged failures to observe the rule, and claims that any asserted *Richards* justification for a no-knock entry....The cost of entering this lottery would be small, but the jackpot enormous: suppression of all evidence, amounting in many cases to a get-out-of-jail-free card. Courts would experience as never before the reality that "[t]he exclusionary rule frequently requires extensive litigation to determine whether particular evidence must be excluded.[190]

The Court also found little benefit in deterrence, a "necessary...[but not] sufficient condition" for applying the exclusionary rule. Ignoring the knock-and-announce requirement, said the Court, would achieve nothing but the destruction of property or physical injury when officers (having a warrant) are

---

[189] *Id.* at 7.
[190] *Id.* at 8.

entitled to enter anyway. The officers thus already have a strong incentive to comply. Even were that not sufficient deterrence, said the Court, not all constitutional violations can or should be deterred by the exclusionary rule (e.g., suppression makes no sense where an already-confessed suspect has his sixth amendment rights violated by thereafter denying him prompt access to counsel). Importantly, the Court, using sweeping language not clearly limited to the case before it, emphasized that legal and cultural changes may have obviated, or at least significantly minimized, the deterrent value of the exclusionary rule today relative to what it was a half-century ago:

> We cannot assume that exclusion in this context is necessary deterrence simply because we found that it was necessary in different contexts and long ago. That would be forcing the public today to pay for the sins and inadequacies of a legal regime that existed almost half a century ago. Dollree Mapp could not turn to 42 U.S.C §1983 for meaningful relief; *Monroe v. Pape*, 365 U.S. 167 (1961), which began the slow but steady expansion of that remedy, was decided the same term as *Mapp*. It would be another 17 years before the §1983 remedy was extended to reach the deep pockets of municipalities…. Citizens whose Fourth Amendment rights were violated by federal officers could not bring suit until 10 years after *Mapp*….

> Hudson complains that "it would be very hard to find a lawyer to take a case such as this,"… but 42 U.S.C. §1988(b) answers this objection. Since some civil rights violations would yield damages too small to justify the expense of litigation, Congress has authorized attorney's fees for civil-rights plaintiffs. This remedy was unavailable in the heydays of our exclusionary-rule jurisprudence….The number of public-interest law firms and lawyers who specialize in civil-rights

grievances has [also] greatly expanded.[191]

Furthermore, said the Court, police professionalism has significantly increased over the last few decades, with a new emphasis on discipline, improved training, enhanced citizen review, and the possibility that failure to teach and enforce constitutional requirements can expose municipalities to civil liability. "[W]e now have increasing evidence," the Court insisted, "that police forces across the United States take the constitutional rights of citizens seriously." The Court was further unpersuaded that the few published decisions announcing huge damages awards for knock-and-announce violations suggested such suits were not succeeding, for "we do not know how many claims have been settled, or indeed how many violations have occurred that produced anything more than nominal injury." The cost-benefit analysis thus weighed squarely against suppression.

Although a majority of the Court supported the attenuation and cost-benefit analyses, only a plurality joined in the final part of the Court's opinion on the independent source doctrine (Justice Kennedy refused to join this portion). The plurality relied on Segura, where, you will recall, police had entered an apartment without a warrant or consent and remained there for 19 hours awaiting a search warrant. Once the warrant had been obtained, the police conducted the search. The Court refused to apply the exclusionary rule, holding that the valid search with a warrant constituted an "independent source" based on information mentioned in the warrant affidavit that was obtained prior to entering the apartment, thus rendering the search "wholly unrelated" to the prior illegal entry. The Hudson plurality concluded that:

> [I]t would be bizarre to treat more harshly the actions in this case [than those in *Segura*], [for here] the only entry was *with* a warrant. If the probable cause backing a warrant that was issued *later in time* could be an "independent source" for a search that proceeded after the officers illegally entered

---

[191] *Id.* at 10-11.

and waited, a search warrant obtained *before* going in must have at least this much effect.[192]

The plurality also cited dicta in *United States v. Ramirez*, where the Court said, "[D]estruction of property in the course of a search may violate the Fourth Amendment, even though the entry itself is lawful and the fruits of the search are not subject to suppression." The *Ramirez* Court had not found entry by breaking a window illegal but said had it done so, it would have been necessary to determine whether there was a sufficient causal nexus between that breaking and the discovery of guns to warrant suppression. Concluded the *Hudson* plurality: "What clearer expression could there be of the proposition that an impermissible manner of entry does not necessarily trigger the exclusionary rule?"[193]

Justice Kennedy, though concurring in the attenuation and cost-benefit portions of the Court's opinion, was apparently sufficiently troubled by that opinion's tone to issue this caution:

> [T]he continued operation of the exclusionary rule, as settled and defined by our precedents, is not in doubt. Today's decision determines only that in the specific context of the knock-and-announce requirement, a violation is not sufficiently related to the later discovery of evidence to justify suppression.
>
> As to the basic right in question, privacy and security in the home are central to the Fourth Amendment's guarantees as explained in our decisions and as understood since the beginnings of the Republic. This common understanding ensures respect for the law and allegiance to our institutions, and it is an instrument for transmitting our Constitution to later generations undiminished in meaning and force. It bears repeating that it is a

---

[192] *Id.* at 14.
[193] *Id.* at 15-16.

serious matter if law enforcement officers violate the sanctity of the home by ignoring the requisites of lawful entry. Security must not be subject to erosion by indifference or contempt.[194]

Kennedy also raised the tantalizing prospect that affirmative evidence offered of a "demonstrated [widespread] pattern of knock-and-announce violations" might be "grave cause for concern," "particularly if those violations were committed against persons who lacked the means or voice to mount an effective protest...." At the same time, he conceded that even were such evidence offered, to allow suppression to return as a remedy would require substantial revisions in the causation requirement "that limits our discretion in applying the exclusionary rule" and would raise difficult practical implications.

Dissenting Justices Breyer, Stevens, Souter, and Ginsburg characterized the majority's decision as "a significant departure from the Court's precedents." First, argued the dissent, the Court had misconceived the nature of the injury done, for more was at stake than physical injury to body or property or the chance to prepare oneself. In particular, the dissent cited with approval this language from the 120 year old case, *Boyd v. United States*, which declared that the Fourth Amendment's prohibitions apply:

> "to all invasions on the part of the government and its employees of the sanctity of a man's home and the privacies of his life. It is not the breaking of his doors, and the rummaging of his drawers, that constitutes the essence of the offence; but it is the invasion of his indefeasible right of personal security, personal liberty and private property."[195]

The costs of the exclusionary rule cited by the majority, said the dissent, are ones general to the rule itself and not specific to the knock-and-announce situation. In fact, the availability of "no-knock warrants" in many states can help to diminish those

---

[194] 547 U.S. __ , 1 (2006) (Kennedy, J., dissenting)(slip op.)
[195] 547 U.S. __ , 3 (2006) (Breyer, J., dissenting)(slip op.).

costs. Accordingly, "[t]he majority's 'substantial social costs' argument is an argument against the Fourth Amendment's exclusionary principle itself. And it is an argument that this Court, *until now*, has consistently rejected."[196]

The dissent rejected the majority's argument that there was no "but-for" causation, arguing that the majority wrongly separated the manner of entry from the fact of entry and misunderstood the independent source and inevitable discovery doctrines. Those doctrines, argued the dissent, do not address "what *hypothetically could* have happened had the police acted lawfully in the first place" but rather what occurred or would have occurred "*despite* (not simply *in the absence of*) that unlawful behavior ." Complying with the knock-and-announce rule was a necessary condition of police entering the home, and entering the home was a necessary pre-condition to finding and seizing the evidence.

The dissent also rejected the majority's creating a "policy-related variant of the causal connection scheme" that constitutes an unwarranted departure from prior law, in part by its emphasis on the kind of harm caused by the specific Fourth Amendment violation. That there is a violation has always been enough to merit suppression absent well-recognized exceptions. The Court thus adds to the meaning of "attenuation" a new, second meaning in which "the interest protected by the constitutional guarantee that has been violated would not be served by suppression of the evidence obtained." The majority's focus on a narrow set of interests, concluded the dissent:

> First it does not fully describe the constitutional values, purposes, and objectives underlying the knock-and-announce requirement. That rule does help to protect homeowners from damaged doors; it does help to protect occupants from surprise. But it does more than that. It protects the occupants' privacy by assuring them that government agents will not enter their home without complying with those requirements (among others) that diminish the

---

[196] *Id.* at 11.

offensive nature of any such intrusion. Many years ago, Justice Frankfurter wrote for the Court that the "knock at the door,…as a prelude to a search, without authority of law… [i]s inconsistent with the conception of human rights enshrined in [our] history" and Constitution.…How much more offensive when the search takes place without any knock at all.[197]

Additionally, the dissent worried that suppression was sorely needed to achieve deterrence. Unlike in other cases where the Court had not worried that an exception to the exclusionary rule would undermine deterrence because police could not in advance count on the assumption that the exception would be available, officers will now "almost always know that they can ignore the knock-and-announce requirement without risking the suppression of evidence discovered after their unlawful entry." Relatedly, the cases reporting violations are "legion," something that alone should be sufficient to meet Justice Kennedy's concern that a "widespread pattern" be shown. Moreover, Michigan's amici "concede that civil immunities prevent tort law from being an effective substitute for the exclusionary rule at this time," civil actions also being "expensive, time-consuming, not readily available, and rarely successful."

For the dissent, precedent supported only two well-recognized exceptions to the exclusionary rule, one where there was specific reason to believe the rule would not achieve appreciable deterrence, notably the good faith and impeachment exceptions as examples, a second where admissibility occurred in proceedings other than criminal trials. The second exception did not apply because this was a criminal case. The first exception did not apply both because there was a need for deterrence generally and because these officers had not acted in good faith because they did not act as a "'reasonable officer would and should act in similar circumstances'"

---

[197] *Id.* at 17-18.

Furthermore, said the dissent, although there may be areas "where text or history or tradition leaves room for a judicial decision that rests upon little more than an unvarnished judicial instinct," "this is not one of them" because our "Fourth Amendment traditions place high value upon protecting privacy in the home" and assuring that constitutional protections are effective; absent good reason not to give practical reality to these protections via the exclusionary rule, violations must prod exclusion "lest the Amendment 'sound the promise to the ear but break it to the hope.'"[198]

Notes and Questions

1.   We have devoted so much space to the *Hudson* case because of the arguable intimation that four Justices (a plurality consisting of Justices Scalia, Roberts, Thomas, and Alito) are ready to abandon the exclusionary rule entirely or to severely cut back its scope and bite. Certainly the dissenters expressed this worry, and even Justice Kennedy in concurrence seemed concerned that that may be where the plurality plans to go. Is this a fair reading of the plurality's views? Do you think that the Court's arguments support elimination of the exclusionary rule, or do the dissenters have the better argument?

2.   There now seem to be two distinct attenuation doctrines. It is a bit unclear whether the Court's cost-benefit approach is part of its attenuation analysis or something separate. Would the logic of the harm-specific approach prevent suppression in other contexts, for example, if the police obtain a confession as the result of using excessive force to stop a fleeing suspect, should an argument that the confession was obtained in violation of the Fourth Amendment and therefore requires suppression be rejected? Has the *Brown* analysis for attenuation of confessions obtained via Fourth Amendment violations been altered by *Hudson*?

3.   The majority and Justice Kennedy in concurrence seem to demand that the defense produce evidence of a widespread problem before suppression should be allowed, the majority

---

[198] *Id.* at 27.

speculating that there may be many successful civil suits without evidence of such success. Are they right to put the burden of proof on this question on the defense?

4. The dissent seems to see the real injury as one to intangible interests in privacy, security, and liberty. The majority focuses more on physical harm to persons or property or narrow privacy harms from psychologically preparing oneself for an invasion of one's home. Which view makes more sense in a criminal case aimed at vindicating injuries to the public versus a civil case aimed at making injured individuals whole? Is your answer affected by the Fourth Amendment's text purporting to vest rights in "the People"?

5. The Court argues that police professionalism has improved, reducing the need for the exclusionary rule. Is it plausible, however, that the exclusionary rule may account for such increased professionalism and that the absence of the rule might encourage backsliding? Or are there cultural and political forces that would prevent backsliding even without a rule?

6. Are civil and regulatory actions likely to be effective deterrents in the absence of the exclusionary rule? Generally? In the context of the knock-and-announce requirement?

7. What different methods of constitutional interpretation did each opinion use and what different data sources did it rely upon? What respective roles did history play versus concern about future real-world effects?

8. Justice Kennedy thought evidence of widespread injury to those without voice or unable effectively to protest might require a rethinking of the Court's exclusionary rule jurisprudence. Such an approach seems to invite an exploration by the Court of the political forces involved to see who has and who lacks political power effectively to protest against police abuses. Is this concern with the impact of search and seizure practices on the politically powerless an appropriate one for Fourth Amendment analysis, or is it more properly limited to places where it has traditionally had more pride of place, such as under the Fourteenth Amendment? Is such a sharp separation between the two amendments viable?

9. Is the dissent right that the plurality has altered the independent source and inevitable discovery doctrines by imagining what the police might do or might have done rather than looking to what they have in fact done? If yes, might that expand those doctrines so much that they swallow much of what remains of the exclusionary rule? Could this be why Justice Kennedy hesitated to join the independent source/inevitable discovery portion of the Court's opinion?

III. EXCEPTIONS TO THE EXCLUSIONARY RULE

A. THE GOOD FAITH EXCEPTION

Page 566. Insert the following after the two-paragraph excerpt from _Massachusetts v. Sheppard_:

In _Groh v. Ramirez_[199], a majority of the Court held that an officer's execution of a warrant that failed to list the particulars of what was to be searched for and seized, and failed to incorporate by reference its supporting application, would not satisfy the good faith exception. Writing for the Court, Justice Stevens began by pointing out that, in contrast to the situation in _Sheppard_, here the officer himself had prepared the warrant and knew that it was defective when he submitted it to the magistrate:

> In _Massachusetts v. Sheppard_, we suggested that "the judge, not the police officers," may have committed "[a]n error of constitutional dimension," because the judge had assured the officers requesting the warrant that he would take the steps necessary to conform the warrant to constitutional

---

[199] 540 U.S. 551 (2004). The pertinent issue in _Groh_ was whether, in a lawsuit under 42 U.S.C. § 1983, the officer was entitled to qualified immunity when he conducted an illegal search, but that analysis is identical to the _Leon_ good faith analysis. _Id._

requirements. Thus, "it was not unreasonable for the police in [that] case to rely on the judge's assurances that the warrant authorized the search they had requested." In this case, by contrast, petitioner did not alert the Magistrate to the defect in the warrant that petitioner had drafted .....

Stevens went on to observe, citing *Leon*, "Nor would it have been reasonable for petitioner to rely on a warrant that was so patently defective, even if the Magistrate was aware of the deficiency." He explained:

> Given that the particularity requirement is set forth in the text of the Constitution, no reasonable officer could believe that a warrant that plainly did not comply with that requirement was valid. Moreover, because petitioner himself prepared the invalid warrant, he may not argue that he reasonably relied on the Magistrate's assurance that the warrant contained an adequate description of the things to be seized and was therefore valid. *Cf. Sheppard*. In fact, the guidelines of petitioner's own department placed him on notice that he might be liable for executing a manifestly invalid warrant. An ATF directive in force at the time of this search warned: "Special agents are liable if they exceed their authority while executing a search warrant and must be sure that a search warrant is sufficient on its face even when issued by a magistrate." Searches and Examinations, ATF Order O 3220.1(7)(d) (Feb. 13, 1997). *See also id.*, at 3220.1(23)(b) ("If any error or deficiency is discovered and there is a reasonable probability that it will invalidate the warrant, such warrant shall not be executed. The search shall be postponed until a satisfactory warrant has been obtained"). And even a cursory reading of the warrant in this case—perhaps just a simple glance—would have revealed a glaring deficiency that any reasonable police officer would have known was constitutionally fatal.

No reasonable officer could claim to be unaware of the basic rule, well established by our cases, that, absent consent or exigency, a warrantless search of the home is presumptively unconstitutional. Indeed, as we noted nearly 20 years ago in *Sheppard*: "The uniformly applied rule is that a search conducted pursuant to a warrant that fails to conform to the particularity requirement of the Fourth Amendment is unconstitutional." Because not a word in any of our cases would suggest to a reasonable officer that this case fits within any exception to that fundamental tenet, petitioner is asking us, in effect, to craft a new exception. Absent any support for such an exception in our cases, he cannot reasonably have relied on an expectation that we would do so.

Petitioner contends that the search in this case was the product, at worst, of a lack of due care, and that our case law requires more than negligent behavior before depriving an official of qualified immunity. But as we observed in [*Leon*,] the companion case to *Sheppard*, "a warrant may be so facially deficient—i.e., in failing to particularize the place to be searched or the things to be seized—that the executing officers cannot reasonably presume it to be valid." This is such a case.

Justice Kennedy disagreed with the majority's application of the *Leon* test. Kennedy believed the officer's reliance on the warrant to be reasonable because the failure was merely a clerical one—in other words, a mistake of fact:

... The central question is whether someone in the officer's position could reasonably but mistakenly conclude that his conduct complied with the Fourth Amendment.

An officer might reach such a mistaken

conclusion for several reasons. He may be unaware of existing law and how it should be applied. Alternatively, he may misunderstand important facts about the search and assess the legality of his conduct based on that misunderstanding. Finally, an officer may misunderstand elements of both the facts and the law. Our qualified immunity doctrine applies regardless of whether the officer's error is a mistake of law, a mistake of fact, or a mistake based on mixed questions of law and fact.

The present case involves a straightforward mistake of fact. Although the Court does not acknowledge it directly, it is obvious from the record below that the officer simply made a clerical error when he filled out the proposed warrant and offered it to the Magistrate Judge. The officer used the proper description of the property to be seized when he completed the affidavit. He also used the proper description in the accompanying application. When he typed up the description a third time for the proposed warrant, however, the officer accidentally entered a description of the place to be searched in the part of the warrant form that called for a description of the property to be seized. No one noticed the error before the search was executed. Although the record is not entirely clear on this point, the mistake apparently remained undiscovered until the day after the search when respondents' attorney reviewed the warrant for defects. The officer, being unaware of his mistake, did not rely on it in any way. It is uncontested that the officer trained the search team and executed the warrant based on his mistaken belief that the warrant contained the proper description of the items to be seized.

The question is whether the officer's mistaken belief that the warrant contained the proper language was a reasonable belief. In my

129

view, it was. A law enforcement officer charged with leading a team to execute a search warrant for illegal weapons must fulfill a number of serious responsibilities. The officer must establish probable cause to believe the crime has been committed and that evidence is likely to be found at the place to be searched; must articulate specific items that can be seized, and a specific place to be searched; must obtain the warrant from a magistrate judge; and must instruct a search team to execute the warrant within the time allowed by the warrant. The officer must also oversee the execution of the warrant in a way that protects officer safety, directs a thorough and professional search for the evidence, and avoids unnecessary destruction of property. These difficult and important tasks demand the officer's full attention in the heat of an ongoing and often dangerous criminal investigation.

An officer who complies fully with all of these duties can be excused for not being aware that he had made a clerical error in the course of filling out the proposed warrant. *See Maryland v. Garrison* (recognizing "the need to allow some latitude for honest mistakes that are made by officers in the dangerous and difficult process of making arrests and executing search warrants"). An officer who drafts an affidavit, types up an application and proposed warrant, and then obtains a judge's approval naturally assumes that he has filled out the warrant form correctly. Even if the officer checks over the warrant, he may very well miss a mistake. We all tend toward myopia when looking for our own errors. Every lawyer and every judge can recite examples of documents that they wrote, checked, and double-checked, but that still contained glaring errors. Law enforcement officers are no different. It would be better if the officer recognizes the error, of course. It would be better still if he does not make the mistake in the first place. In the context of an otherwise proper search, however, an officer's failure to recognize his clerical error on a warrant form can be a reasonable mistake.

The Court reaches a different result by construing the officer's error as a mistake of law rather than a mistake of fact. According to the Court, the officer should not receive qualified immunity because "no reasonable officer could believe that a warrant that plainly did not comply with [the particularity] requirement was valid." The majority is surely right that a reasonable officer must know that a defective warrant is invalid. This much is obvious, if not tautological. It is also irrelevant, for the essential question here is whether a reasonable officer in petitioner's position would necessarily know that the warrant had a clerical error in the first place. The issue in this case is whether an officer can reasonably fail to recognize a clerical error, not whether an officer who recognizes a clerical error can reasonably conclude that a defective warrant is legally valid.

The Court gives little attention to this important and difficult question. It receives only two sentences at the very end of the Court's opinion. In the first sentence, the Court quotes dictum from *United States v. Leon*, to the effect that "a warrant may be so facially deficient—i.e., in failing to particularize the place to be searched or the things to be seized—that the executing officers cannot reasonably presume it to be valid." In the second sentence, the Court informs us without explanation that "[t]his is such a case." This reasoning is not convincing.

To understand the passage from *Leon* that the Court relies upon, it helps to recognize that most challenges to defective search warrants arise when officers rely on the defect and conduct a search that should not have occurred. The target of the improper search then brings a civil action challenging the improper search, or, if charges have been filed, moves to suppress the fruits of the search. The inquiry in both instances is whether the officers' reliance on the defect was reasonable. *See, e.g., Garrison* (apartment wrongly searched because the searching officers did not realize that there were two apartments on the third floor and obtained a warrant to search the entire floor); *Arizona v. Evans* (person wrongly arrested and searched because a court employee's clerical error led officer to believe a warrant existed for person's arrest).

The language the Court quotes from *Leon* comes from a discussion of when "an officer [who] has obtained a [defective] warrant and abided by its terms" has acted reasonably. The discussion notes that there are some cases in which "no reasonably well trained officer should rely on the warrant." The passage also includes several examples, among them the one that the Court relies on in this case: "depending on the circumstances of the particular case, a warrant may be so facially deficient—i.e., in failing to particularize the place to be searched or the things to be seized—that the executing officers cannot reasonably presume it to be valid."

The Court interprets this language to mean that a clerical mistake can be so obvious that an officer who fails to recognize the mistake should not receive qualified immunity. Read in context, however, the quoted language is addressed to a quite different issue. The most natural interpretation of the language is that a clerical mistake can be so obvious that the officer cannot reasonably rely on the mistake in the course of executing the warrant. In other words, a defect can be so clear that an officer cannot reasonably "abid[e] by its terms" and execute the warrant as written.

We confront no such issue here, of course. No one suggests that the officer reasonably could have relied on the defective language in the warrant. This is a case about an officer being unaware of a clerical error, not a case about an officer relying on one. The respondents do not make the usual claim that they were injured by a defect that led to an improper search. Rather, they make an unusual claim that they were injured simply because the warrant form did not contain the correct description of the property to be seized, even though no property was seized. The language from *Leon* is not on point.

Our Court has stressed that "the purpose of encouraging recourse to the warrant procedure" can be served best by rejecting overly technical standards when courts review warrants. *Illinois v. Gates*. We have also stressed that qualified immunity "provides ample protection to all but the plainly incompetent or those who knowingly violate the law." The Court's opinion is inconsistent with these principles. Its analysis requires our Nation's police officers to concentrate more on the correctness of paper forms than substantive rights. The Court's new "duty to ensure that the warrant conforms to constitutional requirements" sounds laudable, but would be more at home in a regime of strict liability than within the "ample room for mistaken judgments" that our qualified immunity jurisprudence traditionally provides.

Page 579. Insert the following before Part IV:

D. HABEAS REVIEW OF VIOLATIONS OF THE FOURTH AMENDMENT EXCLUSIONARY RULE

Pursuant to federal habeas corpus statutes,[200] individuals in state or federal custody may file petitions in federal court challenging the constitutionality of judicial rulings that led to their imprisonment.[201] For example, as we will discuss later in this supplement, a person convicted of a crime may seek habeas relief on the ground that the trial court should have excluded an involuntary confession. However, the Supreme Court has restricted the availability of habeas relief for Fourth Amendment violations. In *Stone v. Powell*,[202] it held that a Fourth Amendment exclusionary rule violation may *not* form the basis for habeas relief if the proceedings that resulted in the conviction provided a "full and fair" opportunity to litigate Fourth Amendment claims. The Court's decision was based on a cost-benefit analysis in which it noted the high costs of the exclusionary rule and found, on the benefit side, "no reason to believe ... that the overall educative effect of the exclusionary rule would be appreciably diminished if search and seizure claims could not be raised in federal habeas corpus review."[203]

---

[200] 28 U.S.C. §2254 and 28 U.S.C. §2255.

[201] There are many procedural hurdles to habeas relief that are not relevant to this discussion.

[202] 428 U.S. 465 (1976).

[203] *Stone* involved habeas review of state court convictions under 28 U.S.C. section 2254, but it has been applied to federal convictions as well. *See United States v. Hearst*, 638 F.2d 1190 (9th Cir. 1980), *cert. denied*, 451 U.S. 938 (1981).

CHAPTER 8

CONFESSIONS AND SELF-INCRIMINATION

I. DUE PROCESS AND VOLUNTARINESS

B. THE TOTALITY OF CIRCUMSTANCES TEST AND ITS MULTIPLE GOALS

1. REDUCING THE RISK OF UNRELIABLE CONFESSIONS

Page 593. Insert the following after the sentencing supported by footnote 11:

In a path-breaking study, two false confession scholars have analyzed "125 recent cases of proven interrogation-induced false confessions (i.e., cases in which indisputably innocent individuals confessed to crimes they did not commit) and how these cases were treated by officials in the criminal justice system."[204] Their analysis was an attempt to confirm or dispel prior studies reporting that interrogation-induced false confession are a primary cause of wrongful convictions.[205] Carefully compiling and reviewing information about the 125 documented false confessions, they discovered that 35 percent of those who falsely confessed were convicted, and even of those not convicted, a fourth spent more than a year in pretrial detention before their cases were disposed of and almost 40 percent spent more than seven months in jail before a favorable disposition. The authors concluded,

---

[204] Steven A. Drizin and Richard A. Leo, *The Problem of False Confessions in the Post-DNA World*, 82 N.C. L. REV. 891 (2004).
[205] *Id.* at 920.

... confession evidence is inherently prejudicial and highly damaging to a defendant, even if it is the product of coercive interrogation, even if it is supported by no other evidence, and even if it is ultimately proven false beyond any reasonable doubt. ... [I]n the overwhelming majority of cases that go to trial, confessions (even if they are demonstrably false) almost always seal the defendant's fate—either by leading the innocent defendant to choose to accept a plea bargain or, more commonly, by leading a judge or jury to wrongfully convict the factually innocent defendant. ... It is remarkable that more than four-fifths of the false confessors in our sample who chose to take their case to trial were convicted. To put it another way, if our sample is representative of the underlying population of false confessors in America, a false confessor who chooses to take his case to trial stands more than an 80% chance of conviction, despite the fact that he is officially presumed innocent, that he is in fact innocent, and that there is no reliable evidence confirming or supporting his false confession.[206]

The authors also found that certain populations were especially vulnerable to the problem of false interrogation-induced confessions: juveniles and the mentally ill and retarded.[207]

Page 594. Insert the following before "Allegations of Abuses Mar Murder Cases":

Echoing arguments that have been made since at least the 1930s, Marissa J. Reich and Steven A. Drizin call for an end to the policies of many state and federal law enforcement agencies, which do not require that interrogations be recorded.[208] According

---

[206] *Id.* at 961.

[207] *Id.* at 963-74.

[208] Steven A. Drizin & Marissa J. Reich, *Heeding the Lessons of History: The Need for Mandatory Recording of Police Interrogations to Accurately Assess the Reliability and Voluntariness of Confessions*, 52 DRAKE L. REV. 619 (2004).

to Drizin and Reich, "preventing false confessions, increasing effective administration of criminal justice, and improving relationships between the police and the public ... have consistently served as a foundation for the arguments laid out by the numerous legal scholars and law enforcement officials who have advocated for a rule requiring electronic recordings to be made during all custodial interrogations."

In 1961 Fred E. Inbau, an opponent of recorded interrogations, argued that "the key to a successful interrogation is privacy because it is a necessary precondition to a confession, and without it, suspects would be less likely to confess." For Drizin and Reich, this argument may be losing its persuasiveness "[i]n the post-DNA age ... and particularly in the past decade, as the number of wrongful convictions based on false confessions has continued to climb. ... [I]t is becoming increasingly difficult for jurors to accept the assertions of police officers that they did not tape interrogations because it was not their policy to do so." They conclude: "It is far too early to declare a victory in the war to end police secrecy in the interrogation room. ... One thing, however, is certain: We can no longer afford to ignore the voices of those who have advocated for an end to secrecy in the police interrogation process."

Page 608. Insert the following before Part G:

F-1. DOES TORTURE VIOLATE THE DUE PROCESS CLAUSE?

1. THE QUESTION

For criminal procedure purposes, the importance of the due process "voluntariness" doctrine is that an involuntary confession—one induced through too much coercion—cannot be used against the person in a criminal case. Recall that the doctrine had its inception in *Brown v. Mississippi*, and that the Court there crafted the doctrine as an exclusionary rule prohibiting the use at trial of involuntary statements. Recent events have caused many to ask whether the voluntariness doctrine goes further. Does it prohibit the use of coercive techniques altogether, or just the introduction at trial of the products of those techniques? In other words, does the due process violation take place immediately upon the application of coercion, or does it take place only when the fruits of coercion are introduced in the courtroom?

The question is an important one for several reasons. First, some victims of coercion may not want to rest with the exclusionary remedy. Because constitutional violations are remediable under federal statutes (principally the federal civil rights statute, 42 U.S.C. § 1983), these victims might want to pursue remedies for the harm they suffered at the hands of interrogators. Moreover, some suspects who have been victimized by coercive interrogations never face criminal charges, so the exclusionary rule supplied by the voluntariness doctrine is not available. In the latter camp are suspects detained and interrogated, but never charged, during the aftermath of September 11, 2001.

The question, then, put starkly, is whether torture alone violates the due process clause. The answer remains unclear. Here are some of the pieces of this constitutional puzzle.

2.   SUBSTANTIVE DUE PROCESS

In *Chavez v. Martinez*,[209] the Court confronted an involuntary confession that the government never sought to introduce in a criminal case. The facts of the case were these: Oliverio Martinez sued police officer Ben Chavez under 42 U.S.C. § 1983 after Chavez interrogated him in a hospital emergency room. Martinez had just been shot in the head and body several times by two other officers. His injuries were so severe as to cause permanent blindness and paralysis. From a transcript of the interrogation, it is clear that Martinez was in agony and believed that life-saving measures would be withheld from him unless he talked to Chavez. In the words of Justice Stevens, the interrogation "was the functional equivalent of an attempt to obtain an involuntary confession from a prisoner by torturous methods."

---

[209] 538 U.S. 760 (2003).

Martinez was never charged with a crime arising out of the incidents preceding his injuries, and the government never sought to use his statements against him.

Martinez's suit alleged that Chavez had violated his Fifth and Fourteenth Amendment rights to be free from coercive interrogations. In the lower courts, the case was thought to involve primarily the Fifth Amendment privilege against self-incrimination. In fact, court rulings in the case were eagerly anticipated because they were expected to clarify whether coercive interrogations constitute instant violations of the Fifth Amendment, or whether the privilege against self-incrimination is violated only when statements are introduced at trial. (We will discuss these aspects of the case in a later section of this supplement.) However, the case developed a Fourteenth Amendment substantive due process angle in the Supreme Court. This arose out of the lower court's decision on qualified immunity. Chavez had raised the qualified immunity defense as a shield, claiming that his conduct did not violate "clearly established" rights—as it would have to before he could be liable under § 1983. The trial court granted summary judgment to Martinez on the issue of qualified immunity, and the Ninth Circuit affirmed. Rather than confine its discussion to clearly established Fifth Amendment rights, however, the court also stated that "a police officer violates the Fourteenth Amendment when he obtains a confession by coercive conduct, regardless of whether the confession is subsequently used at trial." The court explained further that "the due process violation caused by coercive behavior of law-enforcement officers in pursuit of a confession is complete with the coercive behavior itself. ... The actual use or attempted use of that coerced statement in a court of law is not necessary to complete the affront to the Constitution."

In the Supreme Court, those words were carefully scrutinized. Did the Ninth Circuit mean that due process was violated merely because the officer had violated the Fifth Amendment privilege against self-incrimination, and therefore also the clause in the Fourteenth Amendment that incorporates the Fifth Amendment against the states? Or did the Ninth Circuit mean something more—that the officer had violated *other* rights clearly established under the Fourteenth Amendment due process clause?

Martinez had not raised the latter claim in front of the Ninth Circuit, but he did brief it in the Supreme Court, and the Court took it on. The justices issued *six* opinions and achieved little consensus, although this much is clear: a majority of the Court reversed the judgment of the Ninth Circuit and remanded on the issue of whether "Martinez may pursue a claim of liability for a substantive due process violation."

Here are the various positions that emerged from the opinions. We offer these with the suggestion that you first review the material in the text on pages 39 and 40 about the incorporation debate:

A. The apparent majority position (written by Justice Thomas): the Fourteenth Amendment due process clause has two aspects: (a) it incorporates various provisions of the Bill of Rights against the states; and (b) it provides a few carefully limited "substantive" rights. The only substantive due process right pertinent to Martinez's case is the right against government conduct that "shocks the conscience," as described in *Rochin v. California* (see page 156 of the text) and *County of Sacramento v. Lewis* (see page 274 of the text). In order for Martinez to make out a claim involving the former kind of protection, he would have to establish that Chavez violated his privilege against self-incrimination (which he was unable to do because a majority of the Court viewed the privilege as arising only at trial, as we will see in a later section of this supplement). In order to invoke substantive due process, he would have to establish that Chavez's conduct shocked the conscience. This, according to Thomas and language from older cases, requires proof of "the most egregious official conduct"—most likely of the sort that was "intended to injure in some way *unjustifiable by any government interest.*"[210] Thomas stated that the record did not support a finding that Chavez's

---

[210] Here Justice Thomas was quoting from *Lewis*. We added the emphasis because the language appears to require a balancing of the government's interests against those of the suspect. Actually, the full language from *Lewis* leaves open the theoretical possibility that even conduct justifiable by government interests may nevertheless shock the conscience: "conduct intended to injure in some way unjustifiable by any government interest is the sort of official action most likely to rise to the conscience-shocking level").

conduct had shocked the conscience. The Chief Justice and Justice Scalia joined this part of Thomas's opinion. In a separate opinion, Justice Souter indicated that he also would apply substantive due process protection in this case only if Chavez's conduct were found to shock the conscience, but he stated that he believed Martinez "has a serious argument in support of such a position" and proposed a remand on that issue (he gained a majority on the remand). Justice Breyer joined Justice Souter's opinion.

Thus, a majority of 5 justices appears to take the position that coerced statements that are not introduced at trial *do* violate constitutional rights, but *only* if the conduct producing them shocks the conscience.

B. Justice Stevens's position: the Fourteenth Amendment due process clause involves two kinds of protections: (a) it protects against government conduct that shocks the conscience; and (b) it protects against government conduct that interferes with rights "implicit in the concept of ordered liberty." "Unusually coercive police interrogation procedures" violate the second standard, which has as one source of protections the rights found in the Fifth Amendment. Martinez's claim under the second standard is strong, because the interrogation through torture constituted "an immediate deprivation of [Martinez's] constitutionally protected interest in liberty." Justice Stevens thus appears to take a broader position than the majority and would supporting a holding that "unusually" coerced statements that are not introduced at trial *do* violate constitutional rights, *regardless* of government interests.

C. The minority position (written by Justice Kennedy): as compared with the Fifth Amendment, the Fourteenth Amendment is broader and "less specific." It protects the "fundamental right to liberty of the person." That right is violated by "the official imposition of severe pain or pressure for purposes of interrogation," and the violation in such a case is immediate. Kennedy recognized that interrogations must accommodate government interests, but he warned that "police should take the necessary steps to ensure that there is neither the fact nor the perception that the declarant's pain is being used to induce the statement against his will." In this case, Martinez's pain was not caused by Chavez, but Martinez demonstrated that the officer "exploited his pain and suffering with the purpose and intent of securing an incriminating statement." That conduct is remediable under § 1983. Justices Stevens and Ginsburg joined Justice Kennedy. Three justices, then, appear to agree that coerced statements that are not introduced at trial *do* violate constitutional rights *if* the government produced them by intentionally manipulating pain.

The upshot of *Chavez v. Martinez* is this: eight justices[211] apparently accept the proposition that substantive due process protects individuals from certain forms of government conduct—at the bare minimum, from government conduct that shocks the conscience. But the "shocks the conscience" test may require victims to establish government conduct that is unjustifiable when viewed in light of any government interests animating it. Moreover, according to some scholars the "shocks the conscience" test is only the first part of the analysis: "[t]he conclusion that a constitutional right has been violated does not end with a finding that the police behavior shocks the conscience. Rather, the analysis only begins there. The Fourteenth Amendment's guarantee that the government will not deprive any person of due process of law, like virtually all constitutional provisions, is not absolute. The government may deprive a person of life, liberty or property if the government has a sufficiently valid justification for doing so."[212]

A coda to the *Martinez* case: we mentioned above that a majority remanded the case to determine whether Martinez's Fourteenth Amendment rights had been violated. On remand the Ninth Circuit answered in the affirmative.[213] Notice how it picked up on Justice Stevens's broader position:

---

[211] Justice O'Connor did not join any of the opinions on the due process issue.

[212] Marcy Strauss, *Torture*, 48 N.Y.L. SCH. L. REV. 201 (2004) (citing Erwin Chemerinsky, CONSTITUTIONAL LAW 700 (2d ed. 2001): "If a right is deemed fundamental [under the due process clause], the Government must present a compelling interest to justify an infringement. Alternatively, if a right is not fundamental, only a legitimate purpose is required for the law to be sustained.").

[213] *Martinez v. City of Oxnard*, 337 F.3d 1091 (9th Cir. 2003).

... We hold that, if the facts as alleged are proven true, [the conduct] did [violate the Fourteenth Amendment]. Accordingly, Chavez is not entitled to qualified immunity on Martinez's Fourteenth Amendment substantive due process claim.

The Fourteenth Amendment's Due Process Clause protects individuals from state action that either "shocks the conscience" or interferes with rights "implicit in the concept of ordered liberty." Martinez alleges that Chavez brutally and incessantly questioned him, after he had been shot in the face, back, and leg and would go on to suffer blindness and partial paralysis, and interfered with his medical treatment while he was "screaming in pain ... and going in and out of consciousness." Chavez allegedly continued this "interrogation" over Martinez's pleas for him to stop so that he could receive treatment. If Martinez's allegations are proven, it would be impossible not to be shocked by Sergeant Chavez's actions. A clearly established right, fundamental to ordered liberty, is freedom from coercive police interrogation. Because, under the facts alleged by Martinez, Chavez violated Martinez's clearly established due process rights, we affirm the district court's denial of qualified immunity to Chavez. The ultimate resolution of the merits of Martinez's Fourteenth Amendment claim will depend upon the resolution of contested facts. We leave that resolution to the district court.

Chavez challenged this holding by filing a petition for writ of certiorari in the Supreme Court. But that petition has been denied.[214]

---

[214] *See* Petition for Certiorari Filed, 72 U.S.L.W. 3643 (April 2, 2004) (No. 03-1381); 124 S.Ct. 2932 (2004) (petition for writ of certiorari denied).

3. FOURTH AMENDMENT PROHIBITION AGAINST UNREASONABLE SEARCHES AND SEIZURES

As we saw in Chapter 3 of the text, members of "the people" have a constitutional right to be free from unreasonable searches and seizures. This right protects against the use of *unreasonable* means—including bodily invasions (which may be searches) and excessive force—to effect searches or seizures, and many litigants have successfully pursued remedies under these doctrines, primarily for the use of excessive force to arrest. Keep in mind three things, however. First, in § 1983 claims, if the Fourth Amendment applies, then substantive due process analysis is precluded, due to the Court's holding in *Graham v. Connor*[215] that in those cases the amendment providing "an explicit textual source of constitutional protection" applies, rather than "the more generalized notion of substantive due process." Second, the interests protected by the Fourth Amendment probably evaporate once a person has been arrested, although the Court in *Graham v. Connor* noted that the issue has not been settled. Some lower courts appear to reason that Fourth Amendment protections end when the seizure is completed; that substantive due process protections apply to pretrial detainees; and that 8th Amendment protections to convicted, imprisoned persons.[216] Third, under the terms of *United States v. Verdugo-Urquidez*,[217] the Fourth Amendment protects only "the people" of the United States—"a class of persons who are part of a national community or who have otherwise developed sufficient connection with this country to be considered part of that community."

Professor Russell D. Covey has argued that compelled custodial interrogations are themselves Fourth Amendment searches, violating privacy interests protected by that amendment. Accordingly, Professor Covey would presumptively permit such non-consensual interrogation only upon issuance of an "interrogation warrant" based upon probable cause to believe that questioning will produce evidence of crime and limiting the scope of the interrogation, subject perhaps to certain exceptions.

---

[215] 490 U.S. 386, 394-95 (1989).
[216] See *Wright v. Whiddon*, 951 F.2d 297 (11th Cir. 1992).
[217] 494 U.S. 259 (1990).

Question: Would this be a suitable solution to the problem of torture? Does it make sense as a constitutional mandate? As a matter of policy? Note that Covey's idea is different from that of the "torture warrant," which would judicially authorize torture under certain conditions and subject to certain limits. Covey's warrant would authorize interrogation but not via torture. Is the torture warrant an acceptable alternative to Professor Covey's approach? Is Professor Covey's position inconsistent with the position of the Court in any of the cases we have earlier cited?

4. EIGHTH AMENDMENT BAN ON CRUEL AND UNUSUAL PUNISHMENTS

The Eighth Amendment protects against cruel and unusual punishments, but that right applies only to persons actually convicted of a crime. The Court stated in *Ingraham v. Wright*[218] that the Eighth Amendment applies "only after the State has complied with constitutional guarantees traditionally associated with criminal prosecutions .... [T]he State does not acquire the power to punish with which the Eighth Amendment is concerned until after it has secured a formal adjudication of guilt in accordance with the due process of law. When the State seeks to impose punishment without such an adjudication, the pertinent constitutional guarantee is the Due Process Clause of the Fourteenth Amendment." Thus, convicted persons who are tortured in prison may sue based on Eighth Amendment doctrines. These require the claimant to "allege and prove the unnecessary and wanton infliction of pain."[219] Again, if the Eighth Amendment applies in a § 1983 case, substantive due process principles will be inapplicable.

5. INTERNATIONAL LAW

International law prohibits torture, and the United States has ratified most of the treaties containing this law, but it is unclear to what extent American courts will enforce it or afford relief for violations of it. Marcy Strauss remarks that "the impact of these

---

[218] 430 U.S. 651, 671-72 n.40 (1977).
[219] *Whitley v. Albers*, 475 U.S. 312 (1986).

treaties on United States interrogation tactics, frankly is seemingly insignificant. Although the treaties, and international law generally, establish important international norms of conduct, there is no real enforcement."[220]

6.   THE PROBLEM OF EXTRATERRITORIALITY

In light of the "war on terrorism" and the war in Iraq, and the corresponding detention and interrogation by United States government agents of hundreds, perhaps of thousands, of people, claims of abuse are increasingly being brought in United States courts involving extraterritorial conduct. Do the constitutional doctrines discussed above apply in those situations? According to Diane Marie Amann, "[j]urisprudence respecting the degree to which U.S. constitutional guarantees apply abroad is, at best, inconsistent."[221] You are already familiar with the holding in *Verdugo-Urquidez* restricting Fourth Amendment protections to members of "the people" of the United States. Further, Amann relates dicta stating that (1) "aliens are not 'entitled to Fifth Amendment rights outside the sovereign territory of the United States'"[222]; and (2) "'certain constitutional protections available to persons inside the United States are unavailable to aliens outside of our geographic borders.'"[223] Amann points out, however, that "[c]ontaining no territorial limitation akin to that in the European Convention, the text of the U.S. Constitution constrains neither the political branches from acting abroad nor the judicial branch from reviewing their actions."[224] Whether the judicial branch will apply the doctrines we discuss above to review extraterritorial actions of the political branches remains to be seen.

---

[220] Marcy Strauss, *Torture*, 48 N.Y.L. SCH. L. REV. at 252.

[221] Diane Marie Amann, *Guantanamo*, 42 COLUM. J. TRANSNAT'L L. 263 (2004).

[222] Here Amann is quoting Chief Justice Rehnquists's opinion in *Verdugo-Urquidez*, 294 U.S. at 269.

[223] Amann's quote is from *Zadvydas v. Davis*, 533 U.S. 678, 693 (2001).

[224] Amann, *supra* note 127, at 314.

II. CUSTODIAL INTERROGATION AND THE MIRANDA DOCTRINE

B. THE MIRANDA DECISION AND INTERPRETIVE CONTROVERSY

2. CRITIZING AND QUESTIONING MIRANDA

c. *"Involuntariness" versus "Compulsion"*

Page 636. Insert the following before "Affirming *Miranda's* Constitutional Status":

Professor Mark A. Godsey argues that the Supreme Court has wrongfully utilized a subjective voluntariness test when determining a confession's admissibility.[225] According to Godsey "confession law should be regulated primarily by the self-incrimination clause [of the Fifth Amendment] rather than by the due process clauses … [and] … the touchstone for confession admissibility under the self-incrimination clause should be compulsion rather than voluntariness." Furthermore, "existing Supreme Court precedent suggests an objective standard that focuses on government conduct rather than the suspect's state of mind when determining the existence of compulsion."

Godsey attempts to lay out a workable test for compulsion that is based on the self-incrimination clause. The first step of this "objective penalties test" is to determine the baseline of the person being interrogated. "This baseline is highly a function of the environment in which the interrogation takes place and the rights the parties are generally allowed in this setting." For example, when officers are interrogating a person in her house, where that person has the right to smoke whenever she wants, the officers can not tell her to stop smoking because that would take away one of

---

[225] Mark A. Godsey, *Rethinking the Involuntary Confession Rule: Toward a Workable Test for Identifying Compelled Self-Incrimination*, 93 CAL. L. REV. 465 (2005).

her rights. Under Godsey's test, impermissible compulsion exists any time an interrogator alters a person's status quo by removing one of his rights as established by the baseline.

Two special circumstances are worth noting. First, although an interrogator's threat is an objective penalty, an offer is not. It may be difficult to determine the difference between the two, but Godsey suggests the simple rule that any offer made by a government actor must be genuine; an interrogator may only offer to do something he would otherwise not have done. For example, an officer may not offer to forego charging a defendant with rape in exchange for a murder confession if that officer did not have enough evidence to charged the defendant with rape. Second, prolonged interrogation can constitute an objective punishment if a reasonable suspect would feel that the questioning restrained his freedom.

3.   AFFIRMING *MIRANDA'S* CONSTITUTIONAL STATUS

Page 640. Insert the following at the end of the page:

In *Miranda* and *Dickerson*, the Court acknowledged that the Fifth Amendment privilege against self-incrimination forbids the use of confessions produced by coercive interrogation techniques and that *Miranda* warnings are constitutionally required in order to dispel the inherent coercion present in the interrogation room. But a majority of the Court has since affirmed that *Miranda* is a prophylactic rule and not part of the "core" of rights embedded within the Fifth Amendment.[226] A majority of the Court also apparently agrees that *Miranda* violations take place only when *Miranda*-violative statements are introduced at trial.[227] In other words, a suspect interrogated without the requisite warnings may not obtain any relief other than exclusion of his statement at trial.[228]

---

[226] *See Chavez v. Martinez*, 538 U.S. 760 (2003); *United States v. Patane*, 542 U.S. 630 (2004); *Missouri v. Seibert*, 542 U.S. 600, 124 S.Ct. 2601 (2004).

[227] *Chavez*, 538 U.S. at 772; *Patane*, 542 U.S. at 639-40.

[228] Two justices pointed out in *Chavez*, however, that "[t]he question whether the absence of *Miranda* warnings may be a basis for a § 1983 action under any circumstances is not before the Court." *Chavez*, 558 U.S. at 779 (Souter, J.,

C. *MIRANDA'S* IMPACT

Page 648. Delete the portion of the paragraph following footnote 79 and insert the following:

Although it had long been unclear whether the failure to provide this notification should result in the exclusion of any subsequent confession, the United States Supreme Court recently held in *Sanchez-Llamas v. Oregon* that suppression is not required.[229]

D. MIRANDA THRESHOLDS: CUSTODY AND INTERROGATION

1. THE DEFINITION OF CUSTODY

Page 652. Insert the following before Problem 8-10:

A majority of a divided Court in *Yarborough v. Alvarado*[230] insisted that the custody inquiry is an objective one and that the suspect's age is not necessarily a factor to be considered. The suspect in that case, Michael Alvarado, was 17 years old at the time he was brought by his parents to a California police station for questioning about a homicide. Alvarado's parents remained in the lobby of the police station while a detective questioned him for about two hours. The detective did not *Mirandize* Alvarado, who ultimately acknowledged having had some involvement in the killing. When the interview was over, the detective escorted him back to where his parents were waiting, and the three drove away. Alvarado was later arrested, charged, and convicted of second-degree murder. The trial court denied his motion to suppress the statements he made during the interview, finding that he had not been in custody. Although state appellate courts and a federal district court (exercising habeas jurisdiction) agreed, the United States Court of Appeals for the Ninth Circuit ordered the conviction reversed, holding that "the state court erred in failing to

---

concurring in judgment), joined by Justice Breyer.

[229] *See Sanchez-Llamas v. Oregon*, 2006 U.S. LEXIS 5177 (2006).

[230] 541 U.S. 652 (2004).

account for Alvarado's youth and inexperience when evaluating whether a reasonable person in his position would have felt free to leave."[231] The Supreme Court overturned the Ninth Circuit's judgment, based primarily on the deferential standard with which federal courts in habeas cases must view state court findings—a standard that we will discuss later in this Supplement. In another portion of its decision, however, the Court went farther, stating that "[t]he *Miranda* custody inquiry is an objective test." The Court explained:

> ... [T]he objective *Miranda* custody inquiry could reasonably be viewed as different from doctrinal tests that depend on the actual mindset of a particular suspect, where we do consider a suspect's age and experience. For example, the voluntariness of a statement is often said to depend on whether "the defendant's will was overborne," *Lynumn*, a question that logically can depend on "the characteristics of the accused." *Schneckloth*. The characteristics of the accused can include the suspect's age, education, and intelligence, as well as a suspect's prior experience with law enforcement. In concluding that there was "no principled reason" why such factors should not also apply to the *Miranda* custody inquiry, the Court of Appeals ignored the argument that the custody inquiry states an objective rule designed to give clear guidance to the police, while consideration of a suspect's individual characteristics—including his age— could be viewed as creating a subjective inquiry. ...
>
> ... In most cases, police officers will not know a suspect's interrogation history. Even if they do, the relationship between a suspect's past experiences and the likelihood a reasonable person with that experience would feel free to leave often will be speculative. True, suspects with prior law enforcement experience may understand police

---

[231] *Id.* at 659-60.

150

procedures and reasonably feel free to leave unless told otherwise. On the other hand, they may view past as prologue and expect another in a string of arrests. We do not ask police officers to consider these contingent psychological factors when deciding whether suspects should be advised of their *Miranda* rights.

Justice O'Connor, a member of the five-person majority, stated in a concurrence that "[t]here may be cases in which a suspect's age will be relevant to the *Miranda* 'custody' inquiry." She went on to observe that "Alvarado was almost 18 years old at the time of his interview. It is difficult to expect police to recognize that a suspect is a juvenile when he is so close to the age of majority."[232] A four-justice dissent argued that the definition of custody "has introduced the concept of a 'reasonable person' to avoid judicial inquiry into subjective states of mind, and to focus the inquiry instead upon objective circumstances that are known to both the officer and the suspect and that are likely relevant to the way a person would understand his situation."[233] In this case, urged the dissent, "Alvarado's youth is an objective circumstance that was known to the police" and should have been considered. We reproduce an excerpt of Justice Breyer's dissenting opinion below because it is the clearest statement yet of what it means to judge someone from the perspective of the "situated reasonable person" in the context of constitutional criminal procedure:

> In my view, Michael Alvarado clearly was "in custody" when the police questioned him (without *Miranda* warnings) about the murder of Francisco Castaneda. To put the question in terms of federal law's well-established legal standards: Would a "reasonable person" in Alvarado's "position" have felt he was "at liberty to terminate the interrogation and leave"? A court must answer this question in light of "all of the circumstances surrounding the interrogation." And the obvious

---

[232] *Id.* at 669 (O'Connor, J., concurring).
[233] *Id.* at 674 (Breyer, J., dissenting).

answer here is "no." ...

What about Alvarado's youth? The fact that Alvarado was 17 helps to show that he was unlikely to have felt free to ignore his parents' request to come to the station. And a 17-year-old is more likely than, say, a 35-year-old, to take a police officer's assertion of authority to keep parents outside the room as an assertion of authority to keep their child inside as well.

The majority suggests that the law might prevent a judge from taking account of the fact that Alvarado was 17. I can find nothing in the law that supports that conclusion. Our cases do instruct lower courts to apply a "reasonable person" standard. But the "reasonable person" standard does not require a court to pretend that Alvarado was a 35- year-old with aging parents whose middle-aged children do what their parents ask only out of respect. Nor does it say that a court should pretend that Alvarado was the statistically determined "average person"—a working, married, 35-year-old white female with a high school degree. See U.S. Dept. of Commerce, Bureau of Census, Statistical Abstract of the United States: 2003 (123d ed.).

Rather, the precise legal definition of "reasonable person" may, depending on legal context, appropriately account for certain personal characteristics. In negligence suits, for example, the question is what would a "reasonable person" do "under the same or similar circumstances." In answering that question, courts enjoy "latitude" and may make "allowance not only for external facts, but sometimes for certain characteristics of the actor himself," including physical disability, youth, or advanced age. W. Keeton, D. Dobbs, R. Keeton, & D. Owen, Prosser and Keeton on Law of Torts § 32, pp. 174-179 (5th ed.1984); see also Restatement

(Third) of Torts § 10, Comment b, pp. 128-130 (Tent. Draft No. 1, Mar. 28, 2001) (all American jurisdictions count a person's childhood as a "relevant circumstance" in negligence determinations). This allowance makes sense in light of the tort standard's recognized purpose: deterrence. Given that purpose, why pretend that a child is an adult or that a blind man can see? See O. Holmes, The Common Law 85-89 (M. Howe ed.1963).

In the present context, that of *Miranda's* "in custody" inquiry, the law has introduced the concept of a "reasonable person" to avoid judicial inquiry into subjective states of mind, and to focus the inquiry instead upon objective circumstances that are known to both the officer and the suspect and that are likely relevant to the way a person would understand his situation. This focus helps to keep *Miranda* a workable rule.

In this case, Alvarado's youth is an objective circumstance that was known to the police. It is not a special quality, but rather a widely shared characteristic that generates commonsense conclusions about behavior and perception. To focus on the circumstance of age in a case like this does not complicate the "in custody" inquiry. And to say that courts should ignore widely shared, objective characteristics, like age, on the ground that only a (large) minority of the population possesses them would produce absurd results, the present instance being a case in point. I am not surprised that the majority points to no case suggesting any such limitation.

Nor am I surprised that the majority makes no real argument at all explaining why any court would believe that the objective fact of a suspect's age could never be relevant. The majority does discuss a suspect's "history with law enforcement"—a bright red herring in the present context where Alvarado's youth (an objective fact) simply helps to show (with the help of a legal presumption) that his appearance at the police station was not voluntary. ...

As I have said, the law in this case is clear. This Court's cases establish that, even if the police do not tell a suspect he is under arrest, do not handcuff him, do not lock him in a cell, and do not threaten him, he may nonetheless reasonably believe he is not free to leave the place of questioning—and thus be in custody for *Miranda* purposes.

Our cases also make clear that to determine how a suspect would have "gaug[ed]" his "freedom of movement," a court must carefully examine "all of the circumstances surrounding the interrogation," including, for example, how long the interrogation lasted (brief and routine or protracted?), how the suspect came to be questioned (voluntarily or against his will?), where the questioning took place (at a police station or in public?), and what the officer communicated to the individual during the interrogation (that he was a suspect? that he was under arrest? that he was free to leave at will?). In the present case, every one of these factors argues—and argues strongly—that Alvarado was in custody for *Miranda* purposes when the police questioned him.

Common sense, and an understanding of the law's basic purpose in this area, are enough to make clear that Alvarado's age—an objective, widely shared characteristic about which the police plainly knew—is also relevant to the inquiry. Unless one is prepared to pretend that Alvarado is someone he is not, a middle-aged gentleman, well versed in police practices, it seems to me clear that the California courts made a serious mistake.

Notes and Questions

1.   One might argue that Justice O'Connor's concurrence and the four-person dissent, taken together, constitute a five-person majority for the proposition that youth *should* be considered if the suspect were substantially underage and the police obviously perceived that fact. But if the majority is to be taken at its word, should age *ever* be a factor in determining whether a reasonable person in the suspect's situation would have felt free to leave?

2.   Can race, gender, or other characteristics, be distinguished from age for purposes of the custody determination? Is there room in the majority's decision for the proposition that some of these characteristics should be considered when determining whether a reasonable person in the suspect's situation would have felt free to leave? What about a person from another country who obviously believes that he or she will not be permitted to leave—if police admit they were aware of that fact, should it make a difference? Are the concerns about inherent coercion, recognized in *Miranda*, present in such a situation? Is the majority really rejecting Justice Breyer's definition of the reasonable man, and, if so, what definition is the majority applying? If not, how does the majority reach a different conclusion than Justice Breyer?

2.   THE DEFINITION OF INTERROGATION

Page 657. Insert the following before Problem 8-17:

In *Hiibel v. Sixth Judicial District Court of Nevada Humboldt County*,[234] the Court faced a related but different sort of question than whether an officer had "interrogated" a suspect. There, an officer arriving on a scene in response to a tip asked a man on the scene for identification. The man refused eleven requests by the officer seeking the man's name. After warning the man that he would be arrested if he continued his refusal, the

---

[234] 542 U.S. 177 (2004).

officer arrested the man, later identified as Larry Dudley Hiibel. Hiibel was charged with, and convicted for, obstructing a public officer's discharge of his duties. The charge was based on a statute requiring persons detained by an officer on reasonable suspicion of a crime to identify themselves by name, though the statute prohibited compelling answers to any other inquiry. Hiibel's challenge to his conviction included an objection that he was compelled to incriminate himself by being required to give his name, thus violating his constitutional privilege against self-incrimination. The Court affirmed the conviction, rejecting this Fifth Amendment claim.

Specifically, the Court concluded that Hiibel's giving his name under these particular circumstances would not "incriminate" him because it would not "furnish a link in the chain of evidence needed to prosecute him."[235] Said the court, "As best we can tell, petitioner refused to identify himself only because he thought his name was none of the officer's business. Even today, petitioner does not explain how the disclosure of his name could have been used against him in a criminal case."[236] The Court continued:

> The narrow scope of the disclosure requirement is also important. One's identity is, by definition, unique; yet it is, in another sense, a universal characteristic. Answering a request to disclose a name is likely to be so insignificant in the scheme of things as to be incriminating only in unusual circumstances. *See Baltimore City Dept. of Social Srvs. v. Bouknight* (suggesting that "fact[s] the State could readily establish" may render "any testimony regarding existence or authenticity [of them] insufficiently incriminating").… In every criminal case, it is known and must be known who has been arrested and who is being tried… Even witnesses who plan to invoke the Fifth Amendment privilege answer when their names are called to the stand. Still, a case may arise where there is a

---

[235] *Id.* at 199.
[236] *Id.*

substantial allegation that furnishing identity at the time of a stop would have given the police a link in the chain of evidence needed to convict the individual of a separate offense. In that case, the court can then consider whether the privilege applies, and, if the Fifth Amendment has been violated, what remedy must follow. We need not resolve these questions here.[237]

Justice Stevens dissented. First, he concluded that Hiibel's revelation of his name was "testimonial," for a "testimonial communication" is "the extortion of information from the accused, the attempt to force him 'to disclose the contents of his own mind.'"[238] Questioning during a *Terry* stop, argued Justice Stevens, unquestionably qualifies as interrogation, so compelled responses to such questions, because they result from extorting information from the suspect, are therefore also testimonial in nature.

Nor would Justice Stevens accept the majority's core argument that Hiibel's compelled disclosure of his name would not have been "incriminating," for, in Stevens' view, one's name can readily provide the necessary link to inculpatory evidence:

> The Court reasons that we should not assume that the disclosure of petitioner's name would be used to incriminate him or that it would furnish a link in a chain of evidence needed to prosecute him…. But why else would an officer ask for it? And why else would the Nevada Legislature require its disclosure only when circumstances "reasonably indicate that the person has committed, is committing, or is about to commit a crime?" If the Court is correct, then petitioner's refusal to cooperate did not impede the police investigation. Indeed, if we accept the predicate for the Court's holding, the statute requires nothing more than a useless invasion of privacy. I think that, on the

---

[237] *Id.*

[238] *Id.* at 194 (Stevens, J., dissenting).

contrary, the Nevada Legislature intended to provide its police officers with a useful law enforcement tool, and that the very existence of the statute demonstrates the value of the information it demands. . . .

A name can provide the key to a broad array of information about the person, particularly in the hands of a police officer with access to a range of law enforcement database. And that information, in turn, can be tremendously useful in a criminal prosecution. It is therefore quite wrong to suggest that a person's identity provides a link in the chain to incriminating evidence "only in unusual circumstances."[239]

NOTES AND QUESTIONS

1.   Under the majority's approach, would the privilege apply if the officer had asked Hiibel—upon penalty of arrest if he refused—to produce his insurance card, which, once produced, would reveal itself to be expired? If the officer instead requested Hiibel's registration card? Would the privilege apply to the officer's insisting, upon penalty of arrest, that Hiibel produce his national identification card, if such cards were distributed to all citizens and required to be produced by national legislation as a means for better fighting the War on Terrorism? Would the precise content of the information electronically contained on such a card (e.g., medical information, social security number, criminal history, visa and passport usage, etc.) affect your answer to this last question? In connection with these questions, consider this *dictum* from the majority opinion:

Respondents urge us to hold that the statements ... [that the statute] requires are nontestimonial, and so outside the Clause's scope. We decline to resolve the case on that basis. "[T]o be testimonial, an

---

[239] *Id.* at 196 (Stevens, J., dissenting).

accused's communication must itself, explicitly or implicitly, relate a factual assertion or disclose information." …. Stating one's name may qualify as an assertion of fact relating to identity. Production of identity documents might meet the definition as well. As we noted in *Hubbell*, acts of production may yield testimony establishing the "existence, authenticity, and custody of items [the police seek]."[240]

By "acts of production," the Court meant, for example, that a document, such as a business record, that you prepared on your own in the course of your everyday life rather than in response to a government command is not a "compelled" communication, therefore not being protected by the privilege. However, if the government compels you, perhaps by a subpoena, to hand over such a document to it, that handing over may be a compelled testimonial communication. Why? Because, simply by turning over the requested document, you admit: (1) that it exists; (2) that it is what the government requested and is therefore authentic; and (3) that it is in your possession, things that might all be incriminating at trial. Consequently, absent immunity for the information revealed by this "act of production," you can use your privilege against self-incrimination to refuse to produce the document, even though the document's contents are not themselves protected by the privilege. Obviously, if the government cannot get the document from you, as a practical matter, it cannot use its contents against you. (The details of the act of production doctrine are discussed further in Chapter 9).

Would you answer any of these questions differently under Justice Stevens' approach?

2. Who had the better argument—the majority or Justice Stevens? Would Justice Stevens's approach create any practical problems for the police? Could it sometimes work against a detainee's interests? What differences, if any, are there in the interpretive methods followed by the majority and Justice Stevens?

---

[240] *Id.* at 189.

Page 672. Insert the following before Problem 8-30:

G.   SCOPE OF THE MIRANDA EXCLUSIONARY RULE

1.   FRUIT OF THE POISONOUS TREE

The Court put speculation about *Oregon v. Elstad* to rest in *United States v. Patane*[241] and *Missouri v. Seibert*,[242] in which it affirmed that the fruit of the poisonous tree doctrine does not apply to police actions that violate *Miranda* but not "core" Fifth Amendment protections. *Patane* involved an unwarned confession followed by the discovery of physical evidence; *Seibert* a successive interrogation substantially similar to *Elstad*. Neither case produced a majority opinion, although majorities were reached on a few propositions.

In *Patane*, the Court, although fractured, mustered a bare majority for the rule that physical evidence obtained from an unwarned confession need not be excluded. The facts in question were these: Samuel Patane violated a restraining order by attempting to contact his ex-girlfriend, and officers who arrested him also wished to question him about his possible illegal possession of a firearm. After his arrest, the officers attempted to give him *Miranda* warnings, but he stated that he knew his rights and they did not complete the warnings. Patane then made inculpatory statements about the firearm, including instructions about where to find it, and was charged with unlawful possession. The government conceded the inadmissibility of his statements but contended that the firearm itself should be admitted. The United States Court of Appeals for the Tenth Circuit rejected the government's position, holding that *Elstad* did not survive *Dickerson*. Applying the fruit of the poisonous tree doctrine, that court held that the firearm should have been excluded.

But the Tenth Circuit's decision was short-lived. In the Supreme Court, five justices agreed that the trial court need not

---

[241] 542 U.S. 630 (2004).
[242] 542 U.S. 600 (2004).

have excluded the firearm. There was no majority, however, as to the rule's rationale. A plurality (comprised of Justice Thomas, who wrote the plurality opinion, Chief Justice Rehnquist, and Justice Scalia) believed that there had been no constitutional violation or even a violation of the *Miranda* rule. Justice Thomas stated that the "core protection afforded by the Self-Incrimination Clause is a prohibition on compelling a criminal defendant to testify against himself at trial." This core protection "cannot be violated by the introduction of nontestimonial evidence obtained as a result of voluntary statements." The plurality also stated that "a mere failure to give *Miranda* warnings does not, by itself, violate a suspect's constitutional rights or even the *Miranda* rule," because violations of the right and the rule take place only when unwarned statements are admitted at trial. Further, "because police cannot violate the Self-Incrimination Clause by taking unwarned though voluntary statements, an exclusionary rule cannot be justified by reference to a deterrence effect on law enforcement" because there is nothing to deter.[243]

The remaining two justices who supported the Court's judgment—Justices Kennedy and O'Connor—urged narrower grounds similar to those underlying the *Elstad* ruling. Justice Kennedy based their concurrence on a "recognition that the concerns underlying [the *Miranda* rule] must be accommodated to other objectives of the criminal justice system"—i.e., truth-seeking. Said Justice Kennedy, "[i]n light of the important probative value of reliable physical evidence, it is doubtful that exclusion can be justified by a deterrence rationale." But he stated that it was unnecessary to decide whether there indeed was "nothing to deter," as the plurality insisted, or whether the failure to give *Miranda* warnings constituted a *Miranda* violation.[244]

Four justices dissented, expressing concerns about law enforcement incentives created by the rule. Said Justice Souter, "[t]here is no way to read this case except as an unjustifiable invitation to law enforcement officers to flout *Miranda* warnings when there may be physical evidence to be gained."[245] In a

---

[243] *Patane,* 542 U.S. at 642 (plurality opinion of Thomas, J.).

[244] *Id.* at 645 (Kennedy, J., concurring).

[245] *Id.* at 647 (Souter, J., dissenting).

separate dissent Justice Breyer said that he would create a rule requiring exclusion of physical evidence obtained as a result of unwarned questioning "unless the failure to provide *Miranda* warnings was in good faith."[246]

Justice Breyer's "good faith" rule was derived from one he first proposed in *Seibert*. In that case, similar to *Elstad*, police had first obtained an unwarned confession and then, after giving *Miranda* warnings, "cover[ed] the same ground a second time."[247] But in a stunning contrast to *Elstad*, in which the police apparently believed that the suspect was not in custody during the first interrogation, the successive interrogation technique in *Seibert* was intentional—the result of a "police protocol" pursuant to which the interrogating officer had been taught to "question first, then give the warnings, and then repeat the question 'until I get the answer that she's already provided once.'"[248] This "question-first" technique, said Justice Souter writing for a four-justice plurality, is designed to undermine the effectiveness of *Miranda* and should be tested on that basis:

> … [W]hen *Miranda* warnings are inserted in the midst of coordinated and continuing interrogation, they are likely to mislead and deprive a defendant of knowledge essential to his ability to understand the nature of his rights and the consequences of abandoning them. By the same token, it would ordinarily be unrealistic to treat two spates of integrated and proximately conducted questioning as independent interrogations subject to independent evaluation simply because *Miranda* warnings formally punctuate them in the middle.

According to the plurality, the "question-first" technique used on Seibert thwarted *Miranda's* effectiveness and his post-warning statements, induced through use of that technique, had to be excluded. The plurality offered this explanation for how courts in future cases can distinguish between the permissible *Elstad*

---

[246] *Id.* at 647 (Breyer, J., dissenting).
[247] *Seibert*, 542 U.S. at 604 (Souter, J., plurality opinion).
[248] *Id.* at 606 (Souter, J., plurality opinion).

situation and the prohibited *Seibert* one:

> ... The inquiry is simply whether the warnings reasonably convey to a suspect his rights as required by *Miranda*. The threshold issue when interrogators question first and warn later is thus whether it would be reasonable to find that in these circumstances the warnings could function "effectively" as *Miranda* requires. Could the warnings effectively advise the suspect that he had a real choice about giving an admissible statement at that juncture? Could they reasonably convey that he could choose to stop talking even if he had talked earlier? For unless the warnings could place a suspect who has just been interrogated in a position to make such an informed choice, there is no practical justification for accepting the formal warnings as compliance with *Miranda*, or for treating the second stage of interrogation as distinct from the first, unwarned and inadmissible statement. ...

> The contrast between *Elstad* and this case reveals a series of relevant facts that bear on whether *Miranda* warnings delivered midstream could be effective enough to accomplish their object: the completeness and detail of the questions and answers in the first round of interrogation, the overlapping content of the two statements, the timing and setting of the first and the second, the continuity of police personnel, and the degree to which the interrogator's questions treated the second round as continuous with the first.[249]

The plurality thus created a multiple-factor objective approach designed to determine whether *Miranda* warnings were likely effective from the suspect's perspective, although one of the plurality's members, Justice Breyer, wrote separately to provide a

---

[249] *Id.* at 611-15 (Souter, J., plurality opinion).

different method of distinguishing *Elstad* from *Seibert*. He would create a rule that would require exclusion of "the 'fruits' of the initial unwarned questioning unless the failure to warn was in good faith," and it was this intent-of-the-officer approach that he repeated in *Patane*.

The plurality's renunciation of the "question-first" technique employed in *Seibert* was bolstered by a separate concurrence by Justice Kennedy, whose opinion can fairly be characterized as a fifth vote for prohibiting that technique and a second vote for applying an intent-based test:

> The technique used in this case distorts the meaning of *Miranda* and furthers no legitimate countervailing interest. The *Miranda* rule would be frustrated were we to allow police to undermine its meaning and effect. ... When an interrogator uses this deliberate, two-step strategy, predicated upon violating *Miranda* during an extended interview, postwarnings statements that are related to the substance of prewarning statements must be excluded absent specific, curative steps.[250]

In a dissent written for four justices, Justice O'Connor reiterated her position in *Elstad* that, because the fruit of the poisonous tree doctrine does not apply to *Miranda* violations, the only appropriate analysis is the voluntariness of the first and second statements.[251]

III. THE SIXTH AMENDMENT RIGHT TO COUNSEL

C. THRESHOLDS: FORMAL CHARGE AND DELIBERATE ELICITATION

---

[250] *Id.* at 622 (Kennedy, J., concurring).
[251] *Id.* at 622-28 (O'Connor, dissenting).

2. DELIBERATE ELICITATION

Page 705. Insert the following before the first full paragraph, which begins with "The *Massiah* doctrine ...":

In *Fellers v. United States*,[252] the Supreme Court held that officers who arrived at John Fellers' home with an arrest warrant and an indictment, and who informed him that "their purpose in coming was to discuss his involvement in the distribution of methamphetamine and his association with certain charged co-conspirators" had deliberately elicited his statements and thus implicated his Sixth Amendment rights. Fellers' statements, which were made outside the presence of counsel and without a waiver of his rights, could not be admitted. The Court declined to decide whether a subsequent statement, made after *Miranda* warnings and waivers, was admissible, or whether the rationale of *Elstad* would apply.

D. INVOKING AND WAIVING SIXTH AMENDMENT RIGHTS

Page 707. Insert the following before the paragraph that begins with "Once the *Massiah* right has been invoked ...":

In *Iowa v. Tovar*,[253] the Supreme Court emphasized that the extent of warnings required by the Sixth Amendment varies according to context. The *Patterson* case, it said, involved the very early stages of a criminal case, where "the full dangers and disadvantages of self-representation ... are less substantial and more obvious to an accused than they are at trial"—correspondingly the warnings could be "less rigorous." At later stages, a more extensive set of warnings and waivers might be required.

---

[252] 540 U.S. 519 (2004).
[253] 541 U.S. 77 (2004).

F. SCOPE OF THE SIXTH AMENDMENT EXCLUSIONARY RULE

Page 713. Insert the following before the final paragraph, which begins with "Another central ...":

The applicability of the fruit of the poisonous tree doctrine to an *Elstad*-like situation was raised, but not decided, in *Fellers v. United States*.[254] There, the Court held that Fellers' Sixth Amendment rights were violated when the trial court admitted statements he made to police who came to his home to arrest him and who told him, without giving him *Miranda* rights, that they were there to discuss his involvement in drug crimes. Their conduct constituted deliberate elicitation, said the Court. But the Court declined to decide whether Fellers' later statements made at the jailhouse after he had waived his rights, could be admitted:

> ... [B]ecause of its erroneous determination that petitioner was not questioned in violation of Sixth Amendment standards, the Court of Appeals improperly conducted its "fruits" analysis under the Fifth Amendment. Specifically, it applied *Elstad* to hold that the admissibility of the jailhouse statements turns solely on whether the statements were "knowingly and voluntarily made." The Court of Appeals did not reach the question whether the Sixth Amendment requires suppression of petitioner's jailhouse statements on the ground that they were the fruits of previous questioning conducted in violation of the Sixth Amendment deliberate-elicitation standard. We have not had occasion to decide whether the rationale of *Elstad* applies when a suspect makes incriminating statements after a knowing and voluntary waiver of his right to counsel notwithstanding earlier police questioning in violation of Sixth Amendment standards. We therefore remand to the Court of

---

[254] 540 U.S. 519 (2004).

Appeals to address this issue in the first instance.[255]

Question: How do you think this issue will be or should be decided?

Page 717. Add the following after Problem 8-48:

IV. CONFESSIONS AND HABEAS PROCEEDINGS

In habeas corpus actions, in which individuals seek collateral federal review of their convictions, courts cannot grant relief on the ground that the Fourth Amendment exclusionary rule should have applied.[256] But this judicially-created limitation does not apply to habeas relief sought for Fifth and Sixth Amendment violations. According to the Court in *Withrow v. Williams*,[257] the Fifth and Sixth Amendments involve "personal trial rights," whereas *Stone* concerned the Fourth Amendment exclusionary rule, which is designed "to deter future constitutional violations" rather than to confer "a personal constitutional right." Thus, habeas relief is potentially available on the ground that a confession was wrongfully admitted in violation of the Fifth or Sixth Amendments.

But Congress has imposed many *statutory* restrictions on habeas relief that affect Fifth and Sixth Amendment claims. For example, in the Anti-terrorism and Effective Death Penalty Act of 1996 ("AEDPA"), Congress restricted the circumstances in which state prisoners can gain habeas relief. Under AEDPA, relief can be granted only in a case in which a state court decision "was based on an unreasonable determination of the facts in light of the evidence presented in the State court proceeding."[258] As one federal judge has explained, this means that "a federal court may not second-guess a state court's fact-finding process unless, after

---

[255] *Id.* at 520.

[256] The limitation, created in *Stone v. Powell*, 428 U.S. 465 (1976), applies if the habeas petitioner had a full and fair opportunity to raise Fourth Amendment claims in trial court.

[257] 507 U.S. 680 (1993).

[258] 28 U.S.C. section 2254(d)(2).

review of the state-court record, it determines that the state court was not merely wrong, but actually unreasonable."[259] Although this standard is a challenging one, petitioners have satisfied it in a number of cases by establishing that a state court: (1) neglected to make required factual finding altogether; (2) made factual findings under an incorrect legal standard; (3) made factual findings without providing an opportunity for a hearing; or (4) obviously misunderstood, misstated, or ignored the record in making factual findings.

Consider the following problem in light of AEDPA's standard for habeas relief:

PROBLEM 8-49

On May 30, Billy Sheldon was riding his bicycle through a beachside area in Long Beach, California when two assailants tried to take it from him. Billy resisted and the assailants fled. Billy then gave chase and the taller of the assailants turned and shot Billy twice, killing him. Three months later, Detectives Raymond and McClain came to suspect that sixteen-year-old Reef Baylor had been involved in the murder. The detectives obtained an arrest warrant and a search warrant for his apartment. On September 1, at 11:30 p.m., the detectives and three other officers executed the warrants. They found the small teen (Reef was 5' 3" tall) asleep on the living room sofa; his mother, who was his only custodial parent, was not home. The five law enforcement agents woke him, guns drawn and flashlights shining. Reef was taken to the top floor of the police station and placed in an interrogation room alone for half an hour. At 12:15 a.m. the next morning, Detectives Raymond and McClain entered the interrogation room and began questioning him. There were no recording devices used during the interrogation. He was given no food, water, or rest, and after almost three hours of questioning, he confessed to the murder. Detective McClain then produced a tape recorder from his blazer pocket and recorded Reef's confession and waiver of his *Miranda* rights. At 3:30 a.m., he was permitted to call attorney Arthur Closs. Reef told Closs about his arrest, interrogation, and the details

---

[259] *Taylor v. Maddox*, 366 F.3d 992, 999 (9th Cir. 2004).

surrounding the interrogation. Closs explained to Reef that he would not be able to represent him since he may be called as a witness in Reef's case.

Before trial, Reef challenged the admissibility of his confession on the grounds that it was coerced and obtained in violation of *Miranda* and *Edwards*. His testimony at the suppression hearing was as follows:

Q: While you were being questioned, did you ask to speak with anyone?

A: I asked to speak with my attorney. I told the detectives that I knew an attorney that I could call to get some advice. They told me no, that it wouldn't be possible.

Q: Did you ask to speak with anyone else?

A: I then asked if I could speak with my mother, if I could call her. They told me, no.

Q: Did you ask to speak to a lawyer?
A: Yes.

Q: Did you ask to speak with a specific lawyer?

A: Yes, I did. Arthur Closs.

Q: Did you have the phone number of Mr. Closs?

A: Yes, I did.

Q: Did you want to talk to the detectives?

A: No, I didn't.

Q: Did you want to talk with Arthur Closs before you talked to the detectives?

A: Yes.

Q: Did you try to do that?

A: Yes, I did. But they wouldn't let me.

Q: Who wouldn't?

A: One of the detectives, I can't remember.

Q: How did they prevent you from doing that?

A: They told me it wouldn't be possible. They told me that they wanted me to tell them what they wanted to hear. They said to tell them what happened, and that then I could use the phone.

Q: After questioning you more, did you still want to speak with Arthur Closs or any lawyer?

A: Several times, I said I wanted to talk to Arthur.

Reef further testified that he confessed to the murder so that he could make a phone call. He said that he started agreeing with everything so that he could make a phone call and clear things up later. Attorney Closs also testified at the suppression hearing, stating that Reef had called him at approximately 4 a.m. on September 2, highly agitated and in tears. He recalled what Reef told him about the details of the interrogation and about his motivation for confessing. Closs's testimony matched Reef's in every respect. Detective Raymond testified at the suppression hearing as well, stating that he did not recall Reef asking for an attorney. Detective Raymond also could not recall Reef asking for his mother.

The trial court denied Reef's motion to suppress his confession, stating only that "I believe Officer Raymond and not the defendant in this case." The recorded confession was played for the jury, which found Reef guilty of first-degree murder. The appellate courts affirmed.

Question: Assume that you represent Reef in a federal habeas action challenging his conviction. How would you argue that Reef is entitled to relief?

Chapter 9

SELF-INCRIMINATION OUTSIDE THE INTERROGATION ROOM

I. GENERAL PRINCIPLES OF FIFTH AMENDMENT PRIVILEGE

D. THRESHOLDS: COMPULSION, INCRIMINATION, TESTIMONY

Page 737. Insert the following before Part E:

According to a recent four-justice plurality opinion by Justice Thomas, there is one more threshold that must be crossed before one encounters the "core" Fifth Amendment right: the actual *use* of a compelled statement in a criminal case.[260] Justice Thomas explained that while a person may assert a Fifth Amendment *privilege* in non-criminal cases, that privilege is a prophylactic rule "designed to safeguard the core constitutional *right* protected by the Self-Incrimination Clause." One consequence of Thomas's distinction between a core constitutional right and its corollary privileges and rules is his insistence that only the core right is cognizable in § 1983 actions. In other words, according to the Thomas, a government actor cannot be sued under § 1983 for a Fifth Amendment violation unless that actor caused a compelled statement to be used against a person in a criminal case. Three justices explicitly disagreed with Justice Thomas's core-versus-corollary position, as well as his ban on § 1983 remedies for violations of corollary privileges and rules.[261] The remaining two

---

[260] *Chavez v. Martinez*, 538 U.S. 760 (2003) (Thomas, J.). The Chief Justice and Justices O'Connor and Scalia joined Justice Thomas's opinion on this point.

[261] *See Chavez v. Martinez*, 538 U.S. 760 (2003) (Kennedy, J., concurring in part and dissenting in part), joined on this point by Justices Stevens and Ginsburg.

Justices appeared to accept Thomas's core-corollary distinction but not his absolute refusal to afford § 1983 remedies for violations of the corollary privileges and rules.

But Justice Kennedy (joined by Justice Stevens) agreed with Justice Thomas that *Miranda* violations are remediable only through an exclusionary remedy.

Chapter 11

THE RIGHT TO COUNSEL

III. EFFECTIVE ASSISTANCE OF COUNSEL

A. THE *STRICKLAND* TEST

Page 833. Insert the following before Part B:

In *Wiggins v. Smith*,[262] the Supreme Court determined that Wiggins successfully made out a claim of ineffectiveness under the *Strickland* test. According to the Court, Wiggins' lawyers in his murder trial had failed to investigate mitigating evidence that they might have presented to the jury in an effort to convince the jury to reject a death sentence. This failure to investigate fell below the standard of reasonable competence. Said the Court:

> Counsel's decision not to expand their [sic] investigation ... fell short of the professional standards that prevailed in Maryland in 1989. As [one of the defense lawyers] acknowledged, standard practice in Maryland in capital cases at the time of Wiggins' trial included the preparation of a social history report. Despite the fact that the Public Defender's office made funds available for the retention of a forensic social worker, counsel chose not to commission such a report. Counsel's conduct similarly fell short of the standards for capital defense work articulated by the American Bar Association (ABA)—standards to which we long have referred as "guides to determining what is reasonable."[263]

---

[262] 539 U.S. 510 (2003).
[263] *Id.* at 522.

On the prejudice prong of the *Strickland* test, the Court determined that the mitigating evidence that Wiggins' lawyers had failed to investigate and discover "is powerful," that a reasonably competent attorney would have introduced it at sentencing, and that "had the jury been confronted with this considerable mitigating evidence, there is a reasonable probability that it would have returned with a different sentence."[264]

The Court found another occasion to reverse a capital sentence on *Strickland* grounds in *Rompilla v. Beard*.[265] There, Rompilla's attorneys failed to investigate the file of his prior conviction, which they knew the prosecution would use in arguing for the death penalty. No reasonable lawyer, according to the Court, would have neglected such an investigation. Moreover, Rompilla was prejudiced by the unreasonable investigation because the file would have revealed mitigating evidence about Rompilla's childhood and mental health. This evidence "might well have influenced the jury's appraisal" of Rompilla's culpability. Without it, his mitigation case was "a few naked pleas for mercy."

Page 839. Insert the following before "Notes and Questions":

In *Florida v. Nixon*, the United States Supreme Court held that the Florida Supreme Court erred when it applied *Cronic* to a case in which a capital defender conceded his client's guilt in order to focus attention on sentencing issues.[266] The Court stated that unlike a guilty plea, a concession of guilt allows a defendant to retain the rights afforded by a criminal trial. Moreover, because the defendant retained and used those rights, the concession did not rank as a "fail[ure] to function in any meaningful sense as the government's adversary." Finally, the Court made it clear that a capital defendant's express consent is not required before defense counsel can concede guilt because "the gravity of the potential sentence in a capital trial and the proceeding's two-phase structure vitally affect counsel's strategic calculus." But consent may be required from a non-capital defendant: "such a concession in a run-

---

[264] *Id.* at 539.
[265] 545 U.S. 374 (2005).
[266] 543 U.S. 175 (2004).

of-the-mine trial might present a closer question."

Page 840. Insert the following just before Problem 11-1.

4. Remember that the Sixth Amendment provides that "in all criminal prosecutions, the accused shall enjoy the right ... to have the Assistance of Counsel for his defense."[267] Additionally, the Sixth Amendment guarantees the right of the defendant "to be represented by an otherwise qualified attorney whom that defendant can afford to hire, or who is willing to represent the defendant even though he is with funds."[268] However, if a court rejects a criminal defendant's choice of trial counsel, does that rejection constitute a Sixth Amendment violation? Does the Sixth Amendment right to counsel in criminal prosecutions include the right to counsel of one's choice?

Yes, according to the Court's recent decision in *United States v. Cuauhtemoc Gonzalez-Lopez*.[269] There, Gonzalez-Lopez hired an attorney to represent him on a federal conspiracy to distribute (more than 100 kilograms of) marijuana drug charge. The court rejected his counsel of choice and the attorney's application for admission *pro hac vice*, as well as preventing counsel of choice from meeting or consulting with Gonzalez-Lopez on the ground that the attorney violated a state rule of professional responsibility regarding communication with represented parties. In *Gonzalez-Lopez*, the Court clarified the difference between the Constitutional guarantees of a fair trial through the Due Process Clauses and the basic elements of a fair trial, "largely through the several provisions of the Sixth Amendment, including the Counsel Clause." Specifically, the Sixth Amendment right to counsel of choice "commands, not that a trial be fair, but that a particular guarantee of fairness be provided – to wit, that the accused be defended by the counsel he believes to be best:"

---

[267] U.S. CONSTITUTION, Amend. VI.
[268] *Caplin & Drysdale, Chartered v. United States*, 491 U.S. 617, 624-625 (1989).
[269] 2006 U.S. LEXIS 5165 (June 26, 2006).

[t]he right to select counsel of one's choice ... has never been derived from the Sixth Amendment's purpose of ensuring a fair trial. It has been regarded as the root meaning of the constitutional guarantee....Where the right to be assisted by counsel of one's choice is wrongly denied, therefore, it is unnecessary to conduct an ineffectiveness or prejudice inquiry to establish a Sixth Amendment violation. Deprivation of the right is "complete" when the defendant is erroneously prevented from being represented by the lawyer he wants, regardless of the quality of the representation he received. To argue otherwise is to confuse the right to counsel of choice – which is the right to a particular lawyer regardless of comparative effectiveness – with the right to effective counsel – which imposes a baseline requirement of competence on whatever lawyer is chosen or appointed.

An erroneous governmental deprivation of the right to counsel of one's choice (conceded by the government here) constitutes a "structural defect," *i.e.,* one that affects "the framework within which the trial proceeds, and ... [is] not simply an error in the trial process itself."[270] The Supreme Court had "little trouble" concluding that erroneous deprivation of the right to counsel of choice unquestionably qualifies as structural error which, unlike trial error, requires reversal of the accused's conviction without being subjected to a harmless error analysis:

[d]ifferent attorneys will pursue different strategies with regard to investigation and discovery, development of the theory of the defense, selection of the jury, presentation of the witnesses, and style of witness examination and jury argument. And the

---

[270] "Trial error" is the other type of constitutional error and consists of miscues which occur "during presentation of the case to the jury ... and their effect may be quantitatively assessed in the context of other evidence presented in order to determine whether [they were] harmless beyond a reasonable doubt.." *Id.* at *17 (internal quotation marks omitted).

choice of attorney will affect whether and on what terms the defendant cooperates with the prosecution, plea bargains, or decides instead to go to trial [if at all]. It is impossible to know what different choices the rejected counsel would have made, and then to quantify the impact of those different choices on the outcome of the proceedings.... Harmless-error analysis in such a context would be a speculative inquiry into what might have occurred in an alternate universe....

Justices Alito, Kennedy, Thomas, and the Chief Justice dissented. At a minimum, they would require that a defendant "make at least some showing that the trial court's erroneous ruling adversely affected the quality of assistance that the defendant received."

C. THE WORKLOAD PROBLEM

Page 850. Insert the following before Problem 11-2:

Forty years after the Supreme Court decided *Gideon v. Wainwright*, the American Bar Association's Standing Committee on Legal Aid and Indigent Defendants [SCLAID] held a series of public hearings to examine whether *Gideon's* promise of equal justice for the poor is being kept.[271] The testimony of diverse witnesses from all geographic parts of the U.S. supported "the disturbing conclusion that thousands of persons are processed through America's courts every year either with no lawyer at all or with a lawyer who does not have the time, resources, or in some cases the inclination to provide effective representation." The report outlines the nine main findings made by SCLAID:

1) Forty years after *Gideon v. Wainright*, indigent defense in the United States remains in a state of crisis, resulting in a system that lacks fundamental

---

[271] Standing Comm. on Legal Aid & Indigent Defendants, Am. Bar Ass'n, *Gideon's Broken Promise: America's Continuing Quest for Equal Justice* (2004).

fairness and places poor persons at constant risk of wrongful conviction.

2) Funding for indigent defense services is shamefully inadequate.

3) Lawyers who provide representation in indigent defense systems sometimes violate their professional duties by failing to furnish competent representation.

4) Lawyers are not provided in numerous proceedings in which a right to counsel exists in accordance with the Constitution and/or state law. Too often, prosecutors seek to obtain waivers of counsel and guilty pleas from unrepresented accused persons, while judges accept and sometimes even encourage waivers of counsel that are not knowing, voluntary, intelligent, and on the record.

5) Judges and elected officials often exercise undue influence over indigent defense attorneys, threatening the professional independence of the defense function.

6) Indigent defense systems frequently lack basic oversight and accountability, impairing the provision of the uniform, quality services.

7) Efforts to reform indigent defense systems have been most successful when they involve multi-faceted approaches and representatives from a broad spectrum of interests.

8) The organized bar too often has failed to provide the requisite leadership in the indigent defense area.

9) Model approaches to providing quality indigent defense services exist in this country, but these

models often are not adequately funded and cannot be replicated elsewhere absent sufficient financial support.

SCLAID also offered several recommendations that may help correct the failures of the indigent defense systems. Among other things, SCLAID suggested increased state and federal funding, decreased caseloads for indigent defense attorneys, and the creation of "oversight organizations that ensure the delivery of independent, uniform, quality indigent defense representation."